SECOND EDITION

TOUCHSTONE

WORKBOOK 3

MICHAEL MCCARTHY
JEANNE MCCARTEN
HELEN SANDIFORD

CAMBRIDGE
UNIVERSITY PRESS

CAMBRIDGE
UNIVERSITY PRESS

University Printing House, Cambridge CB2 8BS, United Kingdom

One Liberty Plaza, 20th Floor, New York, NY 10006, USA

477 Williamstown Road, Port Melbourne, VIC 3207, Australia

4843/24, 2nd Floor, Ansari Road, Daryaganj, Delhi – 110002, India

79 Anson Road, #06–04/06, Singapore 079906

Cambridge University Press is part of the University of Cambridge.

It furthers the University's mission by disseminating knowledge in the pursuit of education, learning, and research at the highest international levels of excellence.

www.cambridge.org
Information on this title: www.cambridge.org/9781107642713

First published 2005
Second Edition 2014
20 19 18 17 16 15 14 13 12 11 10 9 8

Printed in Malaysia by Vivar Printing

A catalog record for this publication is available from the British Library

ISBN 978-1-107-66583-5 Student's Book
ISBN 978-1-107-62875-5 Student's Book A
ISBN 978-1-107-69446-0 Student's Book B
ISBN 978-1-107-64271-3 Workbook
ISBN 978-1-107-62082-7 Workbook A
ISBN 978-1-107-65147-0 Workbook B
ISBN 978-1-107-62794-9 Full Contact
ISBN 978-1-107-63739-9 Full Contact A
ISBN 978-1-107-63903-4 Full Contact B
ISBN 978-1-107-68094-4 Teacher's Edition with Assessment Audio CD/CD-ROM
ISBN 978-1-107-63179-3 Class Audio CDs (4)

Additional resources for this publication at www.cambridge.org/touchstone2

Contents

The way we are

UNIT 1

Lesson A People in a hurry

1 Opposites

Grammar and vocabulary

Look at the pictures. Correct the sentences to match the pictures.

1. Craig is a careful driver.
   Craig is a reckless driver.

2. Lucia always arrives early.
   ____

3. Carlos is waiting impatiently.
   ____

4. Emily walks slowly.
   ____

5. Laila is talking loudly.
   ____

6. Tom seems polite.
   ____

7. Tamara plays tennis badly.
   ____

8. Joe and Kay are dressed informally.
   ____

2 My new job!

Grammar and vocabulary

Circle the correct words to complete Cleo's email.

New Message

Subject: My new job

Hi Dana,

I started my new job today! But can you believe it? I almost overslept. My alarm always goes off **automatic / automatically**, but today it didn't. Luckily, I woke up early!

I chose my outfit very **careful / carefully** because I wanted to dress **nice / nicely** for my first day. And I didn't want to arrive **late / lately**, so I left home early. I always get **impatient / impatiently** and stressed when the traffic is **slow / slowly**. And then there are all those **reckless / recklessly** drivers! Anyway, I made it to work with no problems.

My boss seems really **serious / seriously**. He likes everyone to do their work **proper / properly**, and he feels **strong / strongly** that everyone needs to get along **good / well**. There was a lot to learn, but he **patient / patiently** explained all my responsibilities. The job is very similar to my old one, but they do things a bit **different / differently** here. He also introduced me to everyone. It's hard to remember all my co-workers' names, but I need to learn them **quick / fast**.

Anyway, the day went by **quick / quickly**, and I'm back home now. I'm really tired, but I can't wait to go back to work tomorrow.

Cleo

3 Are you fast?

Grammar and vocabulary

A Complete the answers with an adjective or adverb. Sometimes more than one answer is possible.

1. A Are you a fast reader?
   B No, actually, I read very *slowly*.
2. A Do you think you're lazy?
   B No, actually, I'm a ______ worker.
3. A Do you have difficulty remembering names?
   B I don't think so. I remember names very ______.
4. A Do you eat your meals quickly?
   B Yes, I'm a ______ eater.
5. A Are you a careful driver?
   B Actually, yes. I drive very ______.
6. A Are you good at sports?
   B Yes, I play most sports ______.

B Write true answers to the questions in part A.

1. *Yes, I am. I read everything very quickly.*
2. ______
3. ______
4. ______
5. ______
6. ______

1 What are they like?

Vocabulary | **A There are eight personality words in the puzzle. Find the other seven. Look in these directions (→↓).**

P	R	A	C	T	I	C	A	L	O	D
D	P	L	O	A	T	B	F	K	S	I
L	O	R	E	L	I	A	B	L	E	S
T	G	T	P	E	B	M	D	W	L	O
A	F	V	J	N	P	C	I	H	F	R
Q	B	I	E	T	S	H	V	N	I	G
H	G	E	N	E	R	O	U	S	S	A
R	K	E	L	D	G	O	K	D	H	N
U	O	U	T	G	O	I	N	G	T	I
O	Y	C	R	L	S	Q	E	Y	I	Z
E	A	S	Y	G	O	I	N	G	Q	E
X	B	A	I	H	P	N	T	A	Z	D

B Complete the sentences with the words from part A.

1. My aunt likes to paint. She has creative ideas and is incredibly *talented* .
2. My sister is totally ____________ . She can never find her car keys and is always losing her cell phone.
3. My friend Steve is extremely down-to-earth and ____________ . He gives useful advice.
4. My brother is really ____________ . He isn't shy at all.
5. My dad bought me a laptop computer for college. He's very kind and ____________ like that.
6. My co-workers are usually good about completing their work. They're fairly ____________ .
7. My mom is pretty laid-back and ____________ . She never gets upset about anything.
8. My little sister never shares anything. She's so ____________ !

2 About you 1

Grammar and vocabulary | **Complete each question with the opposite of the adjective given. Then write true answers.**

1. Are you honest or *dishonest* ? *I'm honest. I always tell the truth.*
2. Is your doctor friendly or ____________ ? ____________
3. Is your best friend reliable or ____________ ? ____________
4. Are you organized or ____________ ? ____________
5. Are you patient or ____________ ? ____________
6. Are your neighbors considerate or ____________ ? ____________

3 All or nothing

Grammar and vocabulary

What's the best next sentence? Circle *a* or *b*.

1. My brother's not talented at all.
   a. He sings, dances, and acts.
   (b.) He can't sing, dance, or act!
2. My parents are extremely generous.
   a. They give a lot of money to charity.
   b. They give a little money to charity.
3. My sister is incredibly smart.
   a. She's the best student in her class.
   b. She does fairly well in school.
4. My best friend is so funny.
   a. His jokes don't make me laugh at all.
   b. His jokes always make me laugh.
5. My cousin is fairly outgoing.
   a. She never goes to parties.
   b. She sometimes goes to parties.
6. My math teacher is really helpful.
   a. She explains things really well.
   b. She can't explain things clearly.
7. My dad is pretty laid-back.
   a. He gets upset about everything.
   b. He doesn't get upset about most things.
8. My brother is completely inconsiderate.
   a. He never helps around the house.
   b. He sometimes helps me around the house.

4 About you 2

Grammar and vocabulary

Use the expressions in the box to write true sentences about someone you know. Then add a second sentence about yourself.

fairly easygoing	not impatient at all	really practical
incredibly friendly	✓ pretty reliable	very honest

1. *My older brother's pretty reliable. I think I'm pretty unreliable.*
2. ______________________________
3. ______________________________
4. ______________________________
5. ______________________________
6. ______________________________

1 They're always . . .

Conversation strategies

The people in this office don't work very hard. Look at the picture, and write what each person is always doing.

1. Jedd *is always leaving work early* .
2. Reba ______ .
3. John ______ .
4. Kayo ______ .
5. Yasmin ______ .
6. Chad ______ .

2 Individual habits

Conversation strategies

Write a response to each statement with *always* and a continuous verb. Use the expressions in the box.

buy things	✓cancel plans	help people	lose stuff	tell jokes

1. Beth is so unreliable. — I know. *She's always canceling plans!*
2. Matt is incredibly disorganized. — That's for sure. ______
3. Elizabeth is very funny. — That's true. ______
4. Theresa isn't practical with money. — You're right. ______
5. Kenny is generous with his time. — Yeah, he is. ______

3 Complaints, complaints

Conversation strategies

Complete each conversation with *always* and a continuous verb. Then add *at least* to the response when appropriate. Write *X* if *at least* is not appropriate.

1. Sam: My sister hardly ever talks to my friends when they come over. She *'s always doing* (do) something else. I mean, she says "Hi," but that's all.
   Fatema: Well, ____________ she isn't rude to them.
2. Jody: Last year, my roommate in college ________________ (borrow) my books and stuff without asking.
   Pam: That's too bad – ____________ it sounds like she was really inconsiderate.
3. Sandy: My last boss was really nice but completely disorganized. She ________________ (cancel) meetings at the last minute.
   Natsuko: Yeah, ____________ it's hard to work for somebody like that.
4. Daniel: My brother ________________ (listen) to music. He's always got his headphones on.
   Sarah: Well, ____________ his music isn't loud.
5. Alejandro: I never see my kids these days. They ________________ (go) to their friends' houses to play basketball or baseball or something.
   Diana: Well, you know, ____________ they're interested in sports. A lot of kids just play computer games all the time.

4 About you

Conversation strategies

Complete each sentence with true information. Use *always* and a continuous verb.

1. When I was little, *I was always eating candy*.
2. My friends and I ________________________________.
3. I have some bad habits. I ________________________________.
4. My best friend ________________________________.
5. My parents ________________________________.
6. My favorite teacher in high school ________________________________.
7. My neighbor ________________________________.

Lesson D Is that a fact?

1 Star qualities

Reading **A Read the article. Circle the two adjectives that describe actor Aishwarya Rai in each column.**

famous	*accomplished*	*inconsiderate*	*generous*
arrogant	*influential*	*down-to-earth*	*unfriendly*
talented	*selfish*	*beautiful*	*nice*

Aishwarya Rai THE QUEEN OF BOLLYWOOD

Aishwarya Rai is the Queen of Bollywood, India's version of Hollywood and the film capital of the world. With over 18,000 websites devoted to her, she is India's, and possibly the world's, best-known actor.

Aishwarya Rai was born in Mangalore, India, on November 1, 1973. She was raised in a traditional, middle-class family. When she was four, her family moved to Mumbai (Bombay), where she still lives today with her husband, actor Abhishek Bachchan, and their daughter, Aaradhya.

Rai started modeling for fun when she was in college studying architecture. She also received many offers to act. However, her first priority was school, so she said no to all movie offers. Then in 1994, at the age of 21, Rai won the title of Miss World. Soon after that, she accepted her first movie role.

Now an accomplished actor, Rai won Filmfare's Award for Best Actress for her role in *Hum Dil De Chuke Sanam* in 2000. She also starred in Bollywood's most successful international blockbuster, *Devdas*.

Rai acts in five different languages: Hindi, Telugu, Tamil, Bengali, and English.

She is the first Bollywood star to be a juror at the Cannes Film Festival in France, to appear in *Rolling Stone* magazine, and to be on *The Oprah Winfrey Show*. Rai is also the first Indian woman to have a statue in London's wax museum, Madame Tussaud's. In 2012, she received the second highest Order of France.

Aishwarya Rai is one of the most beautiful women in the world, but when Oprah Winfrey asked her about her beauty, she simply said, "Beauty is as beauty does," meaning that what you do is more important than how you look. This is perhaps why Rai created a charitable organization called the Aishwarya Rai Foundation, which helps women, children, the elderly, and animals. She was also named the Goodwill Ambassador for a United Nations program on AIDS in 2012. Her philosophy is very simple: "It's nice to be important, but it's important to be nice."

B Read Rai's biography again. Then correct these false sentences.

1. Aishwarya Rai lives ~~by herself~~ *with her husband and daughter* in Mumbai.
2. Rai was born in Mumbai.
3. Rai started modeling in high school.
4. Rai studied acting in college.
5. Rai won the title of Miss World when she was 19.
6. Rai makes movies in four languages.
7. Rai has a statue in Cannes, France.
8. Rai feels that it's important to be beautiful.

2 She's admirable.

Writing **A Use the words and expressions in the box to complete the profile of Midori Goto.**

accomplished	called	started
at the age of	can be	✓was born and raised

Midori Goto

Midori Goto is an incredibly talented violinist. She *was born and raised* in Osaka, Japan. She __________ studying the violin with her mother, and __________ seven, she gave her first public performance in Osaka.

Studying music __________ very demanding, as well as rewarding. When she was only 10, Midori moved to New York City to study music at the Juilliard School. She also attended the Professional Children's School for her academic studies. By the time Midori turned 11, she was already an __________ artist and had performed with the New York Philharmonic.

Midori is also very generous. In 1992, she created an organization __________ Midori & Friends that provides free music education for children in city schools.

Midori is now a professor of music at the University of Southern California.

B Write a short profile about someone you admire.

Unit 1 Progress chart

	What can you do? Mark the boxes. ✓ = I can . . . ? = I need to review how to . . .	To review, go back to these pages in the Student's Book.
Grammar	☐ use manner adverbs and adjectives correctly.	2 and 3
	☐ use regular and irregular adverbs.	3
	☐ use adverbs to make adjectives and adverbs stronger.	5
	☐ add prefixes to adjectives to make opposites.	5
Vocabulary	☐ name at least 12 adverbs.	2, 3, 4, and 5
	☐ name at least 15 personality adjectives.	4 and 5
Conversation strategies	☐ use *always* and a continuous verb to describe individual habits.	6
	☐ use *at least* to point out the positive side of a situation.	7
Writing	☐ write a short profile about someone.	9

Experiences

UNIT 2

Lesson A / Hopes and dreams

1 Have you or haven't you?

Grammar | **A** **Read the "to do" list. What things have you done? What things haven't you done? Write true sentences using the present perfect.**

Things I want to do

1. *drive a sports car*
2. *go skiing*
3. *learn a second language*
4. *see the Taj Mahal*
5. *study photography*
6. *travel to Europe*
7. *try windsurfing*
8. *surf in Hawai'i*

1. *I haven't driven a sports car.*
2. ______
3. ______
4. ______
5. ______
6. ______
7. ______
8. ______

B **Complete the sentences using the present perfect and the expressions in the "to do" list in part A. Use the negative form where necessary.**

1. My cousin *has driven a sports car* once or twice. He loves to drive.
2. My sister and I ______ many times. We love the snow.
3. Each of my brothers ______. One speaks Mandarin and one speaks Cantonese.
4. We ______, but I really want to go to India one day.
5. My teacher ______. She takes beautiful travel photos.
6. My parents ______ before, but they hope to go next year.
7. My older brother ______. He's afraid of the water.
8. My best friend ______, but she wants to go this summer.

2 I've tried . . .

Grammar | **Write sentences with the present perfect.**

1. My teacher (go / many times) to the United States.
   My teacher's been to the United States many times.
   or *My teacher's gone to the United States many times.*
2. My boss (ski / several times) in the Swiss Alps.
   ____
3. I (always / want) to go on a roller coaster.
   ____
4. My neighbor (never / go / before) to Canada.
   ____
5. My parents (see / five times) the movie *Titanic*.
   ____
6. My brothers (try / once or twice) Vietnamese food.
   ____
7. My best friend (never / see) the ocean.
   ____
8. I (never / have) the money to take a vacation.
   ____

3 About you

Grammar | **Answer the questions with true information. Add a frequency expression where necessary.**

1. What's something exciting you've done?
   I've gone hang gliding once.
2. What's something scary you've done?
   ____
3. What's something boring you've done in the last month?
   ____
4. How many times have you been late to class recently?
   ____
5. What country have you always wanted to visit?
   ____
6. What kind of food have you never tried before?
   ____
7. What movie have you seen several times?
   ____
8. What's something you've never done, but always wanted to do?
   ____

1 Have you ever . . . ?

Grammar | **Complete the conversations with the simple past or present perfect.**

1. A *Have* you ever *gone* (go) cliff diving?
   B No, I ________ . It sounds too scary! ________ you ________ (do) it?
   A Yeah, I ________ (go) last weekend.
   B Wow! You're brave. How ________ (be) it?
   A It was incredible! I ________ (love) it.

2. A I ________ never ________ (travel) alone. How about you?
   B No, but I ________ always ________ (want) to. I'm sure it's exciting.
   A I think so, too. Do you know my friend Jill? She ________ (take) a hiking trip alone last year.
   B I know. I ________ (speak) to her about it last week.

3. A ________ you ever ________ (try) horseback riding?
   B Yeah. I actually ________ (do) it once several years ago.
   A Really? ________ you ________ (like) it?
   B No, not really. It ________ (be) very scary.
   A Oh, too bad. I go all the time. I ________ (get) really good at it.

4. A ________ you ________ (do) anything special last weekend?
   B Yes. My family and I ________ (take) a ride in a hot-air balloon! ________ you ever ________ (be) up in one?
   A No, I ________ . ________ you ________ (enjoy) it?
   B Yeah, we ________ (love) every minute! It was amazing!

2 Yes or no?

Grammar and vocabulary

Complete the questions with the simple past or present perfect form of the verbs in the box. Then answer the questions with true information.

break	eat	✓go	have	lose	ride	visit	win

1. *Did* you *go* to the zoo yesterday? *No, I didn't go to the zoo yesterday.*
2. ________ you ever ________ your leg? ________________
3. ________ you ever ________ a spelling contest? ________________
4. ________ you ________ a bike to class yesterday? ________________
5. ________ you ________ your grandparents last summer? ________________
6. ________ you ever ________ a bad cold? ________________
7. ________ you ________ a big breakfast this morning? ________________
8. ________ you ever ________ your wallet? ________________

3 About you

Grammar

Use the cues to write questions in the simple past or present perfect. Then write true answers.

1. (try any new foods on your last vacation)
   Did you try any new foods on your last vacation?
   Yes, I did. I tried oysters. They're delicious.

2. (ever / hike in the mountains)
   ____
   ____
3. (see a lot of movies last summer)
   ____
   ____
4. (ever / walk across a tightrope)
   ____
   ____

5. (ever / find a lost wallet or cell phone)
   ____
   ____
6. (ever / forget an important appointment)
   ____
   ____

1 Tell me more!

Conversation strategies | **Complete the conversations with the responses in the box.**

Cool. Do you have a favorite place?	That sounds great. How do you get there?
I've heard her tests are hard. How did you do?	That's too bad. Did you study for it?
Oh, that sounds hard. Did you finish?	✓Yeah, I am. Do you want to come?

1. **Jake** Hey, Alex! Are you going surfing this weekend?
   Alex *Yeah, I am. Do you want to come?*
   Jake Well, I'm working this weekend. And, actually, I've never surfed before.
   Alex Really? I started surfing three years ago, and now I can't stop.
   Jake ______________________
   Alex Yeah, I like to go to Cove Beach. Have you heard of it?
   Jake Yeah, I have, but I've never been there.
   Alex You should come sometime. I can teach you the basics.
   Jake ______________________
   Alex I usually drive. You can ride your bike there, but it's a little far.
   Jake All right. Tell me the next time you're planning to go.

2. **Ki-Won** Hi, Erin. You look upset. What's wrong?
   Erin I just took Mrs. Chen's English test.
   Ki-Won ______________________
   Erin I don't think I did too well.
   Ki-Won ______________________
   Erin Yeah, I studied really hard.
   Ki-Won Was it an essay or a multiple-choice test?
   Erin Well, it was both. There were 30 multiple-choice questions *and* an essay question!
   Ki-Won ______________________
   Erin Yeah, I finished it, but I didn't have time to check my answers.
   Ki-Won Well, maybe you did better than you think!

2 Did you?

Conversation strategies | **Complete each conversation with a response question to show interest.**

1. A I went on an amazing roller coaster last weekend.
   B *Did you?* That sounds like fun.
2. A I love going to the movies!
   B ____________ Let's go sometime!
3. A I won first prize in the art contest!
   B ____________ That's wonderful!
4. A I'm scared of snakes and spiders.
   B ____________ I am too.
5. A I ride my motorcycle on the weekends.
   B ____________ I've never ridden a motorcycle.
6. A I've broken my arm twice.
   B ____________ That's too bad.
7. A It's my birthday today. I'm 18!
   B ____________ Happy birthday!
8. A I've seen that documentary about fast food four times.
   B ____________ What's it about exactly?

3 Extreme sports

Conversation strategies | **Respond to these statements with a response question. Then add a follow-up question to ask for more information.**

1. In the summer, I love to go hang gliding. — *Do you? Is it scary?*
2. I've gone scuba diving several times. — ____________________
3. Last spring, I went deep-sea fishing. — ____________________
4. I'm a pretty good windsurfer. — ____________________
5. I absolutely love sailing. — ____________________
6. I started surfing last year. — ____________________

Lesson D Travel blogs

1 Finally here!

Reading **A Read Gisele's travel blog about her trip to China. What is one thing she has always wanted to do?**

Gisele's Blog

Finally here!

We arrived in Chengdu, the capital of Sichuan province, the day before yesterday. Exhausted, we went straight to bed, but got up early yesterday. We took a bus to Mount Emei. Fortunately, it's close to Chengdu, so we had a full day to explore. Mount Emei is beautiful, and it has lots of temples and monasteries.

Today we went to Leshan to see the giant Buddha statue. It's the largest stone Buddha in the world and was cut into a cliff. It took 90 years to make. It's huge—233 feet (71 meters) high!

Our hotel in Chengdu is inexpensive and very nice. We met some people from Canada last night. We all went out for some delicious Sichuan food.

We're going to the Giant Panda Nature Reserve tomorrow. I've always wanted to see a baby panda. I'm so excited. Have any of you been there? What's the best way to get there?

Posted January 25 at 7:57 p.m.

JOE TRIP Re: Finally here!

I went to see the pandas last year. It was pretty cool. You're going to love it. There are regular buses from Chengdu, and the bus ride usually takes three hours. But go early to see the pandas when they're awake.

Posted January 25 at 9 p.m.

Last day in Chengdu

We went to the Panda Reserve yesterday. I was able to see some baby pandas. They are so cute. They do amazing things at the Reserve to save these animals.

Posted January 27 at 10 a.m.

Wow!

We just spent a few days in western Sichuan. It was really interesting. Tonight we head to Beijing. I really want to see the Forbidden City, Tiananmen Square, and the Bird's Nest Stadium. This really is a fantastic trip.

Posted February 2 at 4:45 p.m.

B Read the blog again. Then answer the questions.

1. When did Gisele arrive in Chengdu? *She arrived in Chengdu on January 23.*
2. What did she see first? ______
3. Who did she meet at the hotel? ______
4. When does Joe Trip think Gisele should go to see the pandas? ______
5. Where did Gisele go after Chengdu? ______
6. Where is Gisele going tonight? ______

2 Fortunately, . . .

Writing **A Read Ian's blog entry about his trip to Belize. Complete the sentences with *fortunately*, *unfortunately*, or *amazingly*. Sometimes more than one answer is possible.**

Ian's Blog

We were very tired when we got off the plane in Belize City, but *fortunately* , our host was there to meet us. ______________ , the airline lost my luggage, so I left the airport without it. We got on a bus and headed for Maya Mountain Lodge. ______________ , when we got to the lodge, the airline called to say my luggage was on its way. The next morning, we set out on our first day trip. The mountain road was narrow and winding. ______________ , we had a careful driver. Our first stop was at a big waterfall. ______________ , it was raining when we got there, so we just took pictures from the bus. Our next stop was at a river called Rio on Pools. By then it was sunny, so everyone went swimming. ______________ , I didn't have my bathing suit with me, so I couldn't swim. The views were beautiful, and I took a lot of photos. I'm not usually a very good photographer, but ______________ , my pictures turned out really well.

B Write a blog entry about one of the following experiences. Use adverbs like *fortunately* and *amazingly* to show your feelings about what happened.

- Competing in a contest
- Having a fun picnic
- Taking an exciting trip
- Trying a new activity

Blog

____

____

____

____

____

Unit 2 Progress chart

	What can you do? Mark the boxes. ✓ = I can . . . ? = I need to review how to . . .	To review, go back to these pages in the Student's Book.
Grammar	☐ use the present perfect with regular and irregular verbs. ☐ use the present perfect to say what I have and haven't done. ☐ ask and answer questions beginning with *Have you ever . . . ?* ☐ use the simple past to answer questions in the present perfect.	12 and 13 13, 14, and 15 14 and 15 14 and 15
Vocabulary	☐ name at least 12 irregular past participles.	13, 14, and 15
Conversation strategies	☐ keep a conversation going by showing interest. ☐ use *Do you?*, *Did you?*, *Are you?*, or *Have you?* to show interest.	16 17
Writing	☐ use adverbs to show my feelings about something.	19

Wonders of the world

Lesson A / Human wonders

1 That's expensive!

Grammar and vocabulary

Complete the questions with superlatives. Then match the questions with the correct pictures and information below.

1. What's the most expensive (expensive) musical instrument ever sold? h
2. Which country has ____________ (long) school year? ____
3. What sport has ____________ (fans) in the world? ____
4. Who was ____________ (young) number-one classical artist? ____
5. Where's ____________ (narrow) house in the world? ____
6. What's ____________ (famous) statue in the United States? ____
7. What's one of ____________ (tall) hotels in the world? ____
8. What's ____________ (fast) car in the world? ____

a
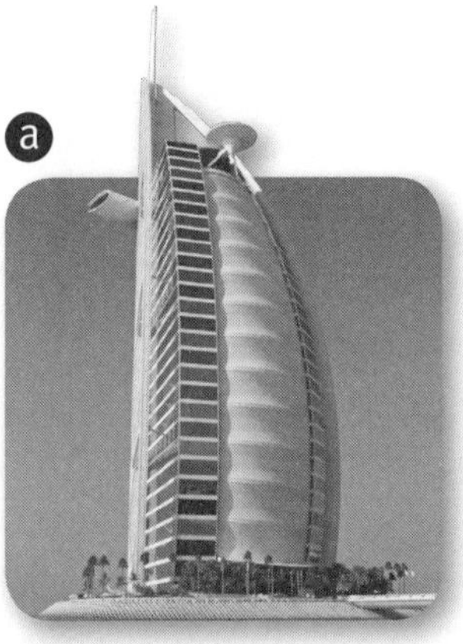
The Burj al-Arab Hotel in Dubai is 321 meters (1,060 feet) tall.

b

Almost 4 million people visit the Statue of Liberty each year.

c

Millions of fans around the world watch soccer.

d

The Thrust SSC went up to 1,227 kilometers (763 miles) per hour.

e

Welsh soprano Charlotte Church was only 12 years old when her album, *Voice of an Angel*, sold over 2 million copies in the UK.

f

Chinese children go to school 251 days a year.

g

The Keret House in Warsaw, Poland, is less than 1.5 meters (5 feet) at its widest point.

h

"The Lady Tennant" violin by Antonio Stradivari sold at auction for over $2 million.

2 It's the best.

Grammar | **Complete the conversations. Use superlative adjectives.**

1. A That's a really big airplane.
   B Yeah. It's *the biggest* airplane I've ever seen.
2. A It's really easy to get to the airport by subway.
   B Right. It's definitely ____________ way to get there.
3. A This restaurant isn't expensive at all.
   B I know. It's ____________ place to eat around here.
4. A This subway is really crowded.
   B Yeah, it is. Actually, it's always ____________ subway line.
5. A Look at that cruise ship. It's so big!
   B It's the *Oasis of the Seas*. It's one of ____________ cruise ships in the world.
6. A Wow. I like your watch. It's so thin.
   B I know. It's ____________ watch I've ever seen.
7. A This is a pretty good price for these pants.
   B Yes, it is. Actually, I think this store has ____________ prices in the mall.
8. A This is a nice gallery, but the new exhibition has some really bad paintings.
   B Yeah. They're some of ____________ paintings I've ever seen.

3 About you

Grammar | **Complete the questions with superlatives. Then write true answers.**

1. Where's *the cheapest* (cheap) place to go shopping around here?
   The cheapest place to go shopping is downtown.
2. And where's ____________ (bad) place to go shopping?
   ____
3. Which neighborhood has ____________ (many) restaurants?
   ____
4. What's ____________ (quiet) neighborhood in your city?
   ____
5. What's ____________ (amazing) building you've ever seen?
   ____
6. Which neighborhood has ____________ (a lot of) traffic?
   ____
7. What's ____________ (wonderful) city you've ever visited?
   ____
8. Where can you buy ____________ (delicious) pastries in your city?
   ____

1 Wonders of the earth

Vocabulary | **A Look at the pictures and complete the puzzle. Then write the answer to the question below.**

1 
2 
3 
4 
5 
6 

1. v o l c a [n] o
2. ___ [ ] ___ ___ ___ ___
3. ___ ___ ___ ___ ___ [ ]
4. ___ ___ [ ] ___ ___ ___ ___ ___
5. ___ ___ ___ ___ ___ ___ [ ]
6. ___ ___ [ ] ___ ___

What is the most powerful force on the planet? Mother N ___ ___ ___ ___ ___ .

B Complete these sentences with the words from part A.

1. The Grand Canyon in Arizona is 1,600 meters (5,249 feet) deep in some parts.
2. The Pacific ________ is about ten times larger than the Arctic.
3. K2, the second highest ________ in the world, is 8,610 meters (28,250 feet) high.
4. In the Sahara ________, temperatures can reach 54 degrees Celsius (130 degrees Fahrenheit).
5. The Siachen, with more than 57 billion cubic meters of ice, is one of the world's largest ________.
6. Mt. Pinatubo in the Philippines is an active ________. It last erupted in 1991.

2 How wide?

Grammar | **Look at the pictures. Complete each question with *How* + adjective. Then write the answers.**

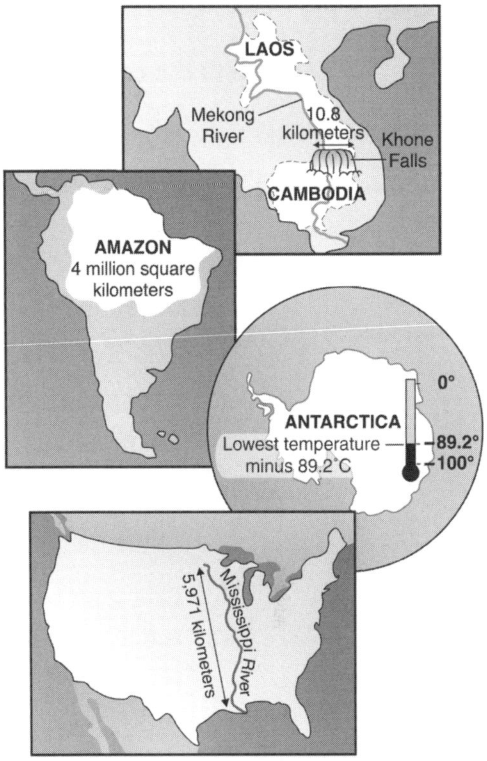

1. Q *How wide* are the Khone Falls on the Mekong River?
   A *They're 10.8 kilometers wide.*
2. Q ____________ is the Amazon Rain Forest?
   A ____________
3. Q ____________ can it get in Antarctica?
   A ____________
4. Q ____________ is the Mississippi River?
   A ____________

3 Discover New Zealand!

Grammar | **Write *How* questions based on the guidebook page. Then answer the questions.**

1. Q *How big is the North Island?*
   A *It's 115,777 square kilometers.*
2. Q ____________
   A ____________
3. Q ____________
   A ____________
4. Q ____________
   A ____________
5. Q ____________
   A ____________
6. Q ____________
   A ____________
7. Q ____________
   A ____________

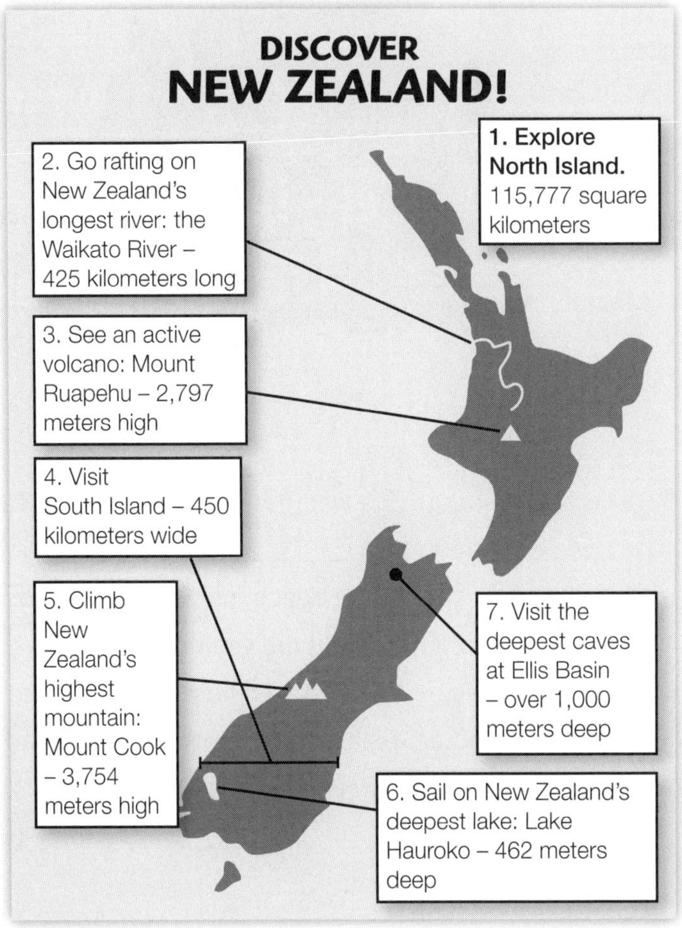

1 Really?

Conversation strategies

A Complete the conversations with the sentences in the box.

It really was.	It sure is.	They really are.	✓Yeah, it really is.
It sure does.	Really? I didn't know that.	We really should.	

1. **Danielle** I think Hawai'i is one of the most interesting states in the U.S.
   Mark *Yeah, it really is.* You know, more than one-third of the world's pineapples are from Hawai'i.
   Danielle Really? I didn't know that. I know it has some of the best surfing in the world, though.
   Mark ______________ They get some of the highest waves there. And did you know all eight islands are volcanoes? . . .

2. **Mee** Mount Sorak in South Korea is so beautiful, especially in the fall.
   Kyong ______________ I love it there. Have you ever gone hiking there?
   Mee Uh-huh, I've hiked there several times with my friends.
   Kyong ______________
   Mee Yeah. The waterfalls are the best.
   Kyong Yeah. ______________

3. **Chika** The weather was terrible last weekend.
   Kacie ______________ I wanted to go to the beach, but it was too cold.
   Chika So what did you do?
   Kacie Well, I stayed home and watched movies.
   Chika Yeah? Well, I heard next weekend's going to be warm and sunny. We should go to the beach then.
   Kacie ______________ Let's plan on going then.

2 The best and the worst!

Conversation strategies

Complete the conversations with superlative adjectives for emphasis.

1. A Chichén Itzá in Mexico has *the coolest* (cool) Mayan ruins. Have you ever been there?
   B Yeah, I had ______ (good) time at the pyramids.
2. A The food at that restaurant was ______ (bad)!
   B I know, but at least the waiter was nice.
3. A How was your weekend?
   B Wonderful! We went to ______ (incredible) lake and rented a boat. We just sailed around for hours!
4. A Have you ever hiked the Appalachian Trail?
   B No, I haven't. But I hear it has ______ (amazing) scenery.

3 It really is the best!

Conversation strategies

You're camping with your friend. Write responses with *really* or *sure* to show you are a supportive listener. Then add a sentence using a superlative adjective for emphasis.

1. It feels really good to be on vacation. — *It sure does! And camping was the coolest idea!*
2. Our hike yesterday was great. — ______
3. We should go swimming in the lake today. — ______
4. It's so nice to be in the country. — ______

4 About you

Conversation strategies

Write true sentences about your last vacation or trip. Use superlative adjectives for emphasis.

1. I went *to Costa Rica last year. They have the most amazing beaches*.
2. I stayed ______.
3. I saw ______.
4. I met ______.
5. I ate ______.
6. I visited ______.

1 The coldest continent

Reading **A Look at the topics below. Then read the article and write the number of the paragraph where the topic is explained in detail.**

3	the driest weather	____	the strongest winds
____	the most time zones	____	the most ice
____	the smallest population	____	the most daylight
____	the farthest south	____	the coldest temperature

AMAZING ANTARCTICA

Vostok Station

1 Antarctica is the coldest, windiest, and driest continent on Earth. It's the fifth largest of the world's seven continents. A layer of ice almost 5 kilometers (3 miles) thick covers the island in some places. In fact, 90% of the world's ice is in Antarctica.

2 The weather in Antarctica is the coldest on Earth. The lowest temperature ever recorded, –89.2 degrees Celsius (–128.6 degrees Fahrenheit), was in 1983 at the Vostok Station, an old Russian research base. At the South Pole, the temperature varies from –35 degrees Celsius (–31 degrees Fahrenheit) in the midsummer to –70 degrees Celsius (–94 degrees Fahrenheit) in the midwinter.

3 Antarctica is not only the world's coldest continent but also the driest place on Earth. Sometimes called the world's largest desert, it gets about the same amount of rain each year as the Sahara. Antarctic winds are the strongest on the planet, reaching up to 320 kilometers (199 miles) per hour.

4 Located at the South Pole, Antarctica is the farthest south of any continent. The South Pole gets six months of nonstop daylight from September through March. Then it gets six months of nonstop darkness. And because it's so far south, Antarctica covers the most time zones – all of them!

5 Explorers first visited Antarctica in 1821. Then in 1899, a Norwegian explorer set up a research station on Antarctica, and for the first time, people could live there. Now there are about 60 research bases there, set up by many different countries. The population of Antarctica grows from about 1,000 in the winter to about 4,000 during the summer. It has the smallest population of any continent.

B Read the article again. Write *T* (true) or *F* (false) for each sentence. Then correct the false sentences.

1. Antarctica is the world's ~~seventh~~ fifth largest continent. F
2. Antarctica has 90% of the world's ice. ____
3. Antarctica gets more rain than the Sahara Desert. ____
4. Antarctica's six months of nonstop daylight begins in March. ____
5. About 1,000 people live in Antarctica during the summer. ____

2 The dry facts

Writing | **A Read the facts about the Sahara. Combine each pair of sentences to form one sentence.**

1	2	3	4
The Sahara is the largest hot desert in the world. It covers 9.1 million square kilometers of land in North Africa.	The sand dunes are the highest dunes in the world. They are the biggest tourist attraction in the Sahara.	The Qattara Depression in Egypt's Sahara is one of the lowest points in Africa. It is 133 meters below sea level.	The Libyan Sahara is the driest place in the desert. It has the least amount of animal or plant life.

1. *The Sahara, the largest hot desert in the world, covers 9.1 million square kilometers of land in North Africa.*
2. ______________________________
3. ______________________________
4. ______________________________

B Write four to six pieces of information about your favorite place. Then combine the facts to make sentences.

Unit 3 Progress chart

	What can you do? Mark the boxes. ✓ = I can . . . ? = I need to review how to . . .	To review, go back to these pages in the Student's Book.
Grammar	☐ use the superlative form of adjectives. ☐ use the superlative with nouns. ☐ ask and answer questions using *how* + adjective.	22 and 23 22 and 23 24 and 25
Vocabulary	☐ name 5 human wonders. ☐ name 5 natural wonders.	21, 22, and 23 21, 24, and 25
Conversation strategies	☐ use short responses with *really* and *sure* to show I'm a supportive listener. ☐ use superlative adjectives to emphasize my opinions or feelings.	26 27
Writing	☐ add information about a place or thing in sentences.	29

Family life

UNIT 4

Lesson A Family gripes

1 Family obligations

Grammar | **Complete the conversations with the correct form of the verbs in the box.**

change	do	help	read	think
clean	do	play	stay	✓watch

1. **Jeff** When I was young, my parents never let me *watch* TV.
   Paul Really? Why not?
   Jeff They wanted me ________ books and ________ about the stories, not just watch TV.
   Paul My parents were pretty easygoing about watching TV.
   Jeff What do you mean?
   Paul Well, they just made me ________ my homework first. Then I could watch all the TV I wanted.

2. **Liz** I heard you broke your arm. What happened?
   Kaya My grandmother asked me ________ a lightbulb in the ceiling fan. I lost my balance and fell off a ladder.
   Liz Ouch! What did your doctor say?
   Kaya He told me ________ home for a week.
   Liz Yeah. And you should get someone ________ you next time.

3. **Kyle** I hate Mondays!
   Naomi Me too. They're the worst.
   Kyle Yeah, Monday is when my mom has me ________ the entire house.
   Naomi Really? By yourself? My brother always helps me ________ my chores.
   Kyle Well, my little sister never helps. My mom just lets her ________ video games all day!
   Naomi That's not fair!

2 Gripes and grumbles

Grammar and vocabulary | **Complete the sentences using the words given.**

1. My brother loves anchovies.
He can't *get me to try one* ______.
(get / try one)

2. My father is pretty strict.
He always ______.
(have / come home early)

3. My parents want me to be a pianist.
They ______.
(make / practice every day)

4. My sister is always watching TV.
She never ______.
(let / have the remote)

5. My daughter is always on her cell phone.
She always ______.
(want / pay the bill)

6. My parents never have enough time to cook.
They often ______.
(ask / prepare dinner)

7. My kids don't like to clean.
They rarely ______.
(help / wash the dishes)

8. My grandfather can't hear very well.
He always ______.
(tell / speak louder)

3 About you

Grammar | **Complete these sentences with true information.**

1. My parents want me *to go to a really competitive college* ______.
2. My best friend often asks me ______.
3. Our English teacher sometimes has us ______.
4. I always tell my friend ______.
5. I can't get my family members ______.
6. Parents shouldn't let their kids ______.
7. My friends sometimes help me ______.
8. I can't make my parents ______.
9. My mom always has me ______.
10. I'm always telling my friend ______.

1 My family tree

Vocabulary | **Look at Kelly's family tree. Then complete the sentences with the words in the box.**

aunt	brother-in-law	great-grandmother	✓immediate	niece	stepmother
blended	cousin	half brothers	nephew	stepdaughter	uncle

1. My sister, Melissa, is the most talented member of my *immediate* family. She's a great musician.
2. My mother's sister, Jessica, is my ________________ . I'm Jessica's favorite ________________ .
3. Jessica's husband, Max, is my mother's ________________ and my ________________ .
4. Max and Jessica's son, Evan, is my ________________ .
5. Evan is my mother's only ________________ .
6. My parents got divorced when I was 12. My father later married Helena. She's my ________________ .
7. My father and his second wife had twin boys, Keith and Noah. They're my ________________ .
8. With Helena, Keith, and Noah, I grew up in a ________________ family.
9. Helena has a daughter from her first marriage. Her name is Kristen. She's my father's ________________ .
10. My ________________ , Irene, is the oldest member of my extended family. She's my grandmother's mother.

2 When I was a kid, . . .

Grammar and vocabulary

Complete the conversation with *used to* or *would* and the verbs given. Sometimes more than one answer is possible.

Tia Hi, Mom. What are you looking at?

Mom I'm looking at some old pictures from when I was a kid.

Tia Cool. Who's this boy?

Mom That's my friend Jay. He *used to live* (live) next door to me.

We *'d spend / used to spend* (spend) every day together in the summer.

Tia Really? Doing what?

Mom We ________ (love) to ride bikes.

We ________ (bring) our lunches and spend the whole day riding in the woods.

Tia Cool. What else?

Mom Well, we ________ (go) fishing, and my mom ________ (always cook) whatever fish we caught.

Tia It sounds like you had a lot of fun.

Mom We did. We ________ (have) an old black-and-white TV, and we ________ (watch) horror movies all the time.

Tia Black-and-white TV? You mean you didn't have a color TV?

Mom No, we didn't. And we didn't have remotes, either.

Tia Wow. I can't even imagine!

3 About you

Grammar

Are these sentences true or false for you? Write *T* (true) or *F* (false). Then correct the false sentences.

1. *F* When I was a kid, I used to go to the movies on Saturdays.
   I didn't use to go to the movies on Saturdays. I would play with my brother.
2. ____ Our neighbors used to have a pet rabbit.
   ____
3. ____ I used to hate pizza.
   ____
4. ____ My parents used to make me go to bed before 9:00.
   ____
5. ____ I used to ride my bike to school every day.
   ____
6. ____ My family used to live in a small house in the country.
   ____

Lesson C / If you ask me, . . .

1 What's your opinion?

Conversation strategies | **Read the news items. Then write your opinions using the expressions in the box.**

I don't think	If you ask me,	It seems to me (that)
I think	It seems like	

The percentage of obese children and adolescents has tripled in the last 30 years.

1. *If you ask me, children and adolescents don't exercise enough these days.*

Learning a language after age 14 is not required in British schools.

2. ______________________________

Surveys show South Korean teens get a new cell phone every year.

3. ______________________________

Most Japanese high schools don't allow their students to hold part-time jobs.

4. ______________________________

Russia has one of the world's highest divorce rates.

5. ______________________________

North American children are spending more time on their computers than they do outside.

6. ______________________________

2 I agree.

Conversation strategies

Follow the instructions and complete the conversations. Use the expressions in the box.

Absolutely.	✓I agree with you.	That's true.
Definitely.	Oh, I know.	You're right.

1. Bruno I think there's a lot of pressure on young couples these days.

   You *I agree with you.*
   (Tell Bruno you agree.)

   Bruno They work longer hours and still don't make much money.

   You ______________________
   (Tell Bruno you're in definite agreement.)

2. Salma If you ask me, our teachers give us too much homework.

   You ______________________ I never have any time to spend with my family.
   (Tell Salma you're in absolute agreement.)

   Salma And we never get a break. We even get homework over school vacations.

   You ______________________
   (Tell Salma she's right.)

3. Ciara It seems like a lot of elderly people live alone.

   You ______________________
   (Tell Ciara her information is true.)

   Ciara It's terrible when families don't spend time with their elderly relatives.

   You ______________________
   (Tell Ciara you know.)

3 Don't you agree?

Conversation strategies

Your friend is telling you his or her opinion. Agree and give an appropriate response.

1. I think even little kids need cell phones these days. — *Definitely. I think they're good in an emergency.*
2. If you ask me, movie tickets cost too much. — ______________________
3. It seems to me that people eat too much fast food. — ______________________
4. I think everyone should learn a second language. — ______________________
5. I don't think people take enough vacation time. — ______________________

Lesson D Family activities

1 Gripes from a stay-at-home dad

Reading **A Read the posts on a social network. What kind of thread is it?**

☐ academic ☐ news ☐ personal ☐ travel

Mark's Page

Mark Santos

What a day! I'm exhausted. I had to nag the kids to get them to help me around the house and clean up because their five cousins are coming for dinner. My brother and sister-in-law are going out for their anniversary. Can you imagine – eight kids for dinner? Also, my aunt wants to come over to see all her great-nieces and -nephews. To top it all off, my wife, Laura, is away on a business trip, so I have to do all the cooking myself. Any ideas for what to make?

One hour ago

Mei-ling Lee Why don't you ask Laura? She's the best cook! Can you get in touch with her?

One hour ago

Mark Santos Right, Mei-ling. Well, right now she's on a flight to Beijing. Before she got this new job, we used to make dinner together most nights. Now that she's working longer hours and traveling more, I guess it's more up to me.

45 minutes ago

Ann Wilkerson Here's an idea: when our kids were younger, we used to make tacos. The kids can help you get everything ready, and then they can make their own. You just need to get everyone to help.

30 minutes ago

Mark Santos Thanks, Ann. That's a great idea. I'll call my brother and have him do some shopping on the way here. I'll get the hang of being a stay-at-home dad pretty soon. Laura's happy traveling, and I'm more of a homebody, so I think it'll work out.

20 minutes ago

B Look at the words and expressions. Find them in the posts, and choose the correct meaning.

1. nag _b_	a. talk loudly	b. ask a lot of times	c. laugh quietly
2. great-niece ____	a. your favorite niece	b. your niece's mother	c. your niece's daughter
3. to top it all off ____	a. the last problem is	b. fortunately	c. one good thing is
4. get the hang of ____	a. stop	b. understand	c. dislike
5. homebody ____	a. someone who doesn't like to go out	b. a housekeeper	c. a personal chef

C Read the posts again. Then answer the questions.

1. How many children does Mark have?
2. How many kids are coming for dinner?
3. Why is his aunt coming over?
4. Who used to do the cooking?
5. What is Mark going to make?

2 Lessons learned

Writing **A Read the journal entry. Then complete the sentences with the expressions in the box.**

In those days	Nowadays	Today	When I was a kid

March 8

I just bought some lemonade from some kids on the corner near my apartment. It brought back so many memories! ________________ , I used to make lemonade with my brother. We'd set up a stand in front of our house and sell the lemonade to people walking down the street. ________________ , we didn't worry about money, and we drank more lemonade than we sold. ________________ , I still remember the lesson that experience taught me – don't drink your profits! I don't think we ever made any money, but it sure was a lot of fun. ________________ we have air conditioning, but I still like a cold cup of lemonade on a hot day.

B Write a journal entry about a childhood memory you remember clearly. Use the expressions from part A.

____

____

____

____

____

____

____

____

Unit 4 Progress chart

	What can you do? Mark the boxes. ✓ = I can . . . ? = I need to review how to . . .	To review, go back to these pages in the Student's Book.
Grammar	☐ use *let*, *make*, *have*, *get*, *want*, *ask*, *tell*, and *help*. ☐ use *used to* and *would* to talk about memories.	34 and 35 36 and 37
Vocabulary	☐ name at least 15 family members.	36
Conversation strategies	☐ give opinions with expressions like *I think* and *It seems to me*. ☐ use expressions like *absolutely*, *exactly*, and *you're right* to agree.	38 39
Writing	☐ use time markers to write about the past and the present.	41

Food choices

UNIT 5

Lesson A Healthy food

1 A bag and a can

Vocabulary | **Look at the pictures. Complete the sentences with the expressions in the box. Some expressions are used more than once.**

a bag of	a box of	a carton of	a package of
a bottle of	a can of	a jar of	

1. In the United States, you can buy *a bottle of* milk or ______________ milk.

2. In Thailand, you can buy ______________ curry paste or ______________ curry paste.

3. In Japan, you can buy ______________ crackers or ______________ crackers.

4. In Australia, you can buy ______________ asparagus or ______________ asparagus.

5. In Colombia, you can buy ______________ coffee or ______________ coffee.

6. In France, you can buy ______________ soup or ______________ soup.

2 What did Selena buy?

Vocabulary | **Look at the picture. Write what Selena bought at the grocery store.**

1. *a jar of olives*
2. ____________
3. ____________
4. ____________
5. ____________
6. ____________
7. ____________
8. ____________

3 A lot or a little?

Grammar | **Carl is doing his weekly grocery shopping. Circle the best quantifier to complete each of his thoughts.**

Hmm . . . we only have **a few** / **a little** cheese left in the refrigerator. I guess I'll get some more. And there's **not many** / **not much** butter left, either, so I'll get some of that, too. I don't think that there are **many** / **much** oranges left in the fruit bowl, and I know my roommate likes bananas, so I'll get both. He's such a picky eater. He eats **very few** / **very little** vegetables, but I should get **a few** / **a little** peppers, at least. Um . . . the ice-cream section . . . I really want to eat **fewer** / **less** ice cream, but maybe I can buy a light, fat-free kind with **fewer** / **less** calories in it. Well, I think that's all I need. . . .

4 About you

Grammar and vocabulary | **Complete each sentence with true information. Use a quantifier from the box and a food word. The quantifiers may be used more than once.**

a few	fewer	very few
a little	less	very little

1. There are *very few apples* in my refrigerator.
2. I try to eat ____________ every day.
3. I had ____________ yesterday.
4. I'm eating ____________ these days.
5. There's ____________ in my cupboard.
6. I eat ____________ than I used to.

1 Prepared foods

Vocabulary | There are ten ways to serve foods in the puzzle. Find the other nine. Look in these directions (→ ↓).

B	A	K	E	D	X	L	Y	Q	B
A	B	L	M	A	R	R	T	E	G
R	O	A	S	T	P	A	I	P	R
B	I	C	M	R	Z	W	Y	I	I
E	L	S	M	O	K	E	D	C	L
C	E	D	C	J	E	L	M	K	L
U	D	F	R	I	E	D	P	L	E
E	Z	T	S	T	E	A	M	E	D
D	M	U	X	P	Y	R	I	D	P

2 Smoked bread?

Vocabulary | Cross out the food that is the least likely to go with the preparation. Then replace it with an appropriate food.

1. smoked – cheese / turkey / ~~bread~~ *fish*

2. raw – fish / ice cream / vegetables

3. boiled – grapes / eggs / potatoes

4. steamed – rice / milk / pizza

5. fried – noodles / yogurt / chicken

6. barbecued – noodles / beef / lamb

7. pickled – cabbage / cucumbers / cheese

3 Too much rice

Grammar | **What's the problem? Complete the sentences with *too*, *too much*, *too many*, or *enough*.**

1. Martha got _too much_ rice and not _enough_ meat.

2. Sheila ate ____________ cupcakes!
   She often eats ____________ dessert.

3. This coffee costs ____________ !
   It's ____________ expensive.

4. Taro drank the lemonade
   ____________ fast.

5. The soup's not hot ____________ .
   And there's ____________ salt in it.

6. Alice didn't take the turkey out early
   ____________ . Now she won't have
   ____________ food for dinner.

4 About you

Grammar and vocabulary | **Complete the questions with *too*, *too much*, *too many*, or *enough*. Then write true answers.**

1. Do you eat a lot of snacks? Do you eat _too many_ ? _I eat three snacks a day._
2. Do you eat ____________ vegetables every day? ____________
3. Do you ever feel ____________ full after eating a meal? ____________
4. Do you exercise ____________ – at least twice a week? ____________
5. Do you eat ____________ for lunch so you don't need a snack later? ____________
6. Do you ever eat meals ____________ quickly and feel sick? ____________
7. Do you drink ____________ water – at least two liters every day? ____________
8. Do you think you eat ____________ fried foods? ____________

Lesson C / Whatever you're having.

1 Either way is fine.

Conversation strategies **Complete the conversation with the expressions in the box.**

either one is fine	whatever you're having
either way is fine	✓whichever is easier for you

Brent I'm going to cook dinner tonight, so what would you like? Chicken or steak?

Imani Well, you're the cook, so *whichever is easier for you* .

Brent No, I want you to choose. I got to decide last night's dinner menu.

Imani Well, you know, I really like both, so ______________ .

Brent OK. I'll cook the chicken. How do you want it tonight? Fried or grilled?

Imani Oh, ______________ . I'm sure whatever you cook will be delicious.

Brent OK, I'll grill it. Now, what do you want to drink?

Imani Oh, ______________ . You know me, anything is fine.

Brent Well, you're certainly easy to please!

Imani I try.

2 Whatever you want.

Conversation strategies **Imagine you are at a friend's house. Respond to each question appropriately to let your friend decide.**

Friend Do you want to eat out or get takeout later tonight?

You *Oh, I don't care. Whatever you prefer.*

Friend OK, let's go out. Do you prefer Mexican or Indian food?

You ______________

Friend Well, I know this great Mexican restaurant. I'll make reservations. 7:00 or 8:00?

You ______________

Friend Oh, let's make it 7:30. Now, should we drive or take the subway?

You ______________

Friend Well, driving is easier, so should we take your car or mine?

You ______________

Friend All right. I'll drive. Now, would you like something to drink? Tea? Coffee?

You ______________

3 I'm OK for now.

Conversation strategies | **Use polite refusal expressions to complete the conversation.**

Peggy Would you like some more iced tea?

Nora *No, thanks. Maybe later.* I've got enough here.

Peggy Gosh, there were a lot of fries here. I still have some left. Would you like a few?

Nora ____________________ I'm trying to cut down on things like fries. You didn't have much salad. Take some of my carrots.

Peggy ____________________ You know, they have the best chocolate cake here. You should try some.

Nora ____________________ I'm trying to eat less sugar, too.

Peggy Oh. Well, are you going to have coffee?

Nora ____________________

4 Let's have some . . .

Conversation strategies | **Respond to each question by politely refusing or letting the other person decide.**

1. Let's have some ice cream. Would you like vanilla or strawberry?

   Either one is fine. Whatever you're having.

2. I'm getting hungry. Do you want something to eat?

   ____

3. There's cake and cookies for dessert. Which would you like?

   ____

4. I'm going to bake a pie. Do you prefer apple or peach?

   ____

5. I'm taking you to lunch today! Would you like Italian or Thai?

   ____

1 Food alternatives

Reading | **A** Read the article. Circle the helpful foods and products that are mentioned.

DOUBLE DUTY

Did you know that you have a personal beauty spa right in your refrigerator? And did you know that for easy fix-it projects around your home, you simply need to look at your grocery list for help? Here are some ways to make your groceries do double duty.

Hair and face care

BRIGHTER EYES Were you up all night studying for a test, and now it's morning, and your eyes are tired and puffy? Take a few slices of a cold cucumber, and place them over your eyes. Leave them on for about 5 to 10 minutes. Good-bye puffiness, good morning bright eyes!

CLEARER SKIN Uh-oh. You've got a date this weekend, and you just woke up with a pimple! Take a little toothpaste – not too much – and put it on the pimple. Leave it on for at least 5 minutes. Repeat daily if necessary. By Saturday night, your date won't notice a thing!

LIGHTER HAIR Do you want some summer highlights and can't afford a hair salon? The next time you're going out in the sun, squeeze some fresh lemon juice into a bowl, and comb it through your hair.

Fix-it projects

WATER STAINS Did you leave a cold glass of water on a wooden table overnight, and now there's a ring on it? You can't make it disappear, but you can lighten it considerably – with toothpaste. Mix equal parts toothpaste and baking soda, and then rub the mixture into the wood with a damp cloth. Wipe it off with a dry cloth.

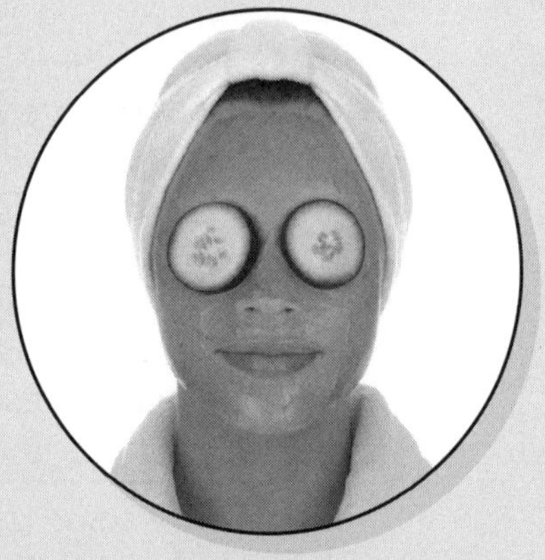

CLOGGED DRAIN Is your shower drain clogged, and now the water's taking a long time to go down? Mix equal parts salt, baking soda, and cream of tartar, and then pour it down the drain. Follow with boiling water. Leave it overnight.

Pest remedy

INSECT BITES One thing about summer you can't control is the bugs. But you can stop them from biting you. White vinegar will deter some pests. Pour some vinegar onto a cloth, and wipe over your skin. The smell goes away after the vinegar has dried, but the bugs won't like the taste of the vinegar. Reapply often.

B Read the article again. Then match the two parts of each sentence.

1. For puffy eyes, _d_
2. To get rid of pimples, ____
3. To lighten your hair, ____
4. To treat a water stain on wood, ____
5. To unclog a drain, ____
6. To deter biting pests, ____

a. wipe vinegar on your skin.
b. put baking soda, cream of tartar, and salt in it.
c. rub toothpaste and baking soda on it.
d. place cucumber slices on them.
e. comb lemon juice through it.
f. put a little toothpaste on them.

2 Ethnic eateries

Writing **A** **Read the article about healthy eating habits in Okinawa. Add *for example*, *like*, or *such as* to introduce examples. Often more than one is correct.**

Food as the Secret to Good Health

If you want to live to be 100 years old, you may want to try the Okinawan diet. People on Okinawa live a very long time. Although Okinawa is part of Japan, the diet is a little different. ____________ , people eat a lot of green vegetables, ____________ broccoli and green beans. In fact, about three quarters of their diet is vegetables, fruit, and whole grains. Only about 3% comes from meat, poultry, and eggs. They also eat more soybean products, ____________ tofu. They don't eat many foods that have a lot of fat, ____________ , cheese.

B **Write an article about healthy foods that people eat in your country. Give examples using *for example*, *like*, and *such as*.**

____

____

____

____

____

____

____

Unit 5 Progress chart

	What can you do? Mark the boxes. ✓ = I can . . . ? = I need to review how to . . .	To review, go back to these pages in the Student's Book.
Grammar	☐ use quantifiers like *a little*, *a few*, *very little*, *very few*, etc.	44 and 45
	☐ use *too*, *too much*, *too many*, and *enough*.	47
Vocabulary	☐ talk about food using expressions like *a jar of*, *a can of*, *a box of*, etc.	43 and 44
	☐ name at least 8 different ways of serving food.	46
Conversation strategies	☐ respond to questions by letting another person decide.	48
	☐ use expressions like *No, thanks. I'm fine* to refuse an offer politely.	49
Writing	☐ use *for example*, *like*, and *such as* to introduce examples.	51

Managing life

UNIT 6

Lesson A / Making plans

1 What are you doing after work?

Grammar | Circle the best verb forms to complete the conversations.

1. Ahmed — Hey, Finn. What **do you do** / **are you doing** after work tonight?
   Finn — I have no plans. **I just go** / **I'm just going home**. Why? What are you up to?
   Ahmed — Well, **I go** / **I'm going** to the gym around 5:00, but after that, I have no plans.
   Finn — OK. Well, maybe **I'm stopping by** / **I'll stop by** later.
   Ahmed — Sure. **I make** / **I'll make** dinner.
   Finn — Oh, no. I just remembered. **I have** / **I'm having** a doctor's appointment at 6:00.
   Ahmed — That's OK. **I'm waiting** / **I'll wait** for you to eat. Just come right over when you're done.
   Finn — All right. **I'm going to be** / **I'll be** there by 7:30.
   Ahmed — Don't be late!

2. Leah — Hi, Mom. I was just calling to let you know that **I take** / **I'm going to take** a 5:30 train this Friday.
   Mom — Great, honey. **I'm meeting** / **I'll meet** you at the station.
   Leah — No, that's OK. **I won't need** / **I'm not needing** you to pick me up. **I get** / **I'll get** a taxi.
   Mom — OK. **Do you bring** / **Are you bringing** your friend?
   Leah — Yeah. Janice **will come** / **is coming** with me.
   Mom — Oh, how nice. I can't wait to meet her!
   Leah — I'm sure **you're going to like** / **you like** her. See you Friday!

2 Let me check my schedule.

Grammar | **Look at Millie's weekly planner, and complete the conversation. Use the verbs in parentheses and the information from the planner.**

Monday ~~art exhibit with Jenna~~	**Thursday** *6:30 guitar lesson, as usual*
Tuesday *6:30 guitar lesson*	**Friday** *plans with Heidi?*
Wednesday *5:45 eye doctor appointment*	**Saturday** *dinner with Greg*
	Sunday *7:00 flight*

Raquel Let's have dinner together this week.
Millie Sounds good. I'd love to catch up with you.
Raquel How about Saturday?
Millie Hmm . . . I can't Saturday. I *'m meeting / 'm going to meet Greg for dinner* (meet).
Raquel Well, then, what about Thursday?
Millie That won't work, either. I ________________ (have).
Raquel Oh, yeah, I forgot. Well, I'm free next Sunday.
Millie Sunday I'm leaving for Dallas. My flight ________________ (leave).
Raquel And Friday?
Millie I may have plans with Heidi.
Raquel Oh? What are you guys doing?
Millie I don't know. I ________________ (call) on Friday to see what's up.
Raquel OK. Well, then why don't *you* pick a day?
Millie Let's see . . . Oh, Wednesday, I ________________ (have). Actually, you know what? Jenna canceled our plans to see an art exhibit tonight. Do you want to go?
Raquel Sure. I ________________ (go) with you!

3 About you

Grammar | **Answer the questions with true information.**

1. What are you going to do tonight?
____
2. Are you doing anything special this weekend?
____
3. Do you have any appointments this month? If yes, who with?
____
4. Who are you having dinner with tomorrow night?
____
5. What do you think you'll do when you finish this exercise?
____

1 Make up your mind.

Vocabulary | **A Complete the *make* and *do* expressions. Use the definitions to help you.**

1. make a *living* = work to earn money
2. make a good ________ = make someone think of you positively
3. make a ________ = make a positive change
4. do your ________ = try your hardest
5. make up your ________ = decide
6. make ________ of = make jokes about and laugh at
7. make ________ = make certain
8. make a ________ = get something wrong
9. do the ________ = figure out the numbers
10. make ________ = seem logical

B Complete the conversations with the *make* and *do* expressions from part A.

1. A Which computer are you going to get? Did you *make up your mind* ?
   B No. I can't decide. I like this one, but it's expensive.
   A Well, buy the best you can afford. It doesn't ________________ to buy a cheap one.
   B Yeah, you're right. I need to ________________ and look at all the numbers before I decide.

2. A Are you all prepared for your interview? You look great. I'm sure you'll ________________ .
   B Thanks. I really want this job with the children's charity. I've always wanted to ________________ in people's lives. I know it's not well paid, but it's how I want to ________________ .
   A Well, good luck. You'd better leave now to ________________ you get there on time.

3. A I have to give a presentation to the class today. I'm so afraid I'll ________________ and say something wrong.
   B Well, just ________________ , and I'm sure everything will be fine.
   A I know. I'm just scared that the other students will ________________ me.

2 Let's ask Daphne.

Grammar | **Circle the best expression to complete each sentence.**

Dear Daphne

Dear Daphne,

I'm not doing well in social studies. My teacher talks really fast in class, and I can't understand what he says. (**I'd rather not**) **/ I don't have to** ask questions in class because I don't want the other kids to make fun of me. But **I'd rather / I've got to** do something because I have a test next week. I don't want to fail it. What should I do?

Miguel

Dear Miguel,

You'd better not / You're going to have to talk to your teacher. He probably doesn't even realize you're having a problem. **You'd better / You'd rather not** make an appointment with him as soon as possible! Good luck!

Daphne

Dear Daphne,

I have a part-time job after school, and so far I've earned about $2,000. My parents think **I'd better not / I ought to** save it for college because I'll need it then. I disagree with them. **I ought to / I'd rather** buy a car with the money. It's my money, and I want to enjoy it, so I think I can do what I want with it. What do you think?

Risa

Dear Risa,

You'd rather / You'd better listen to your parents because college is expensive. It's smart to save money for your education. Plus, I'm sure you'll want to have fun once you're in college, and that requires money. So, **you might want to / you don't have to** put money aside for living expenses. Everything costs a lot these days! Good luck!

Daphne

3 About you

Grammar | **Write true sentences about these topics.**

1. something you've got to do this week
   I've got to make up my mind about a summer job.
2. something you'd better do before next week
   ______
3. two things you don't have to do this week
   ______
4. something you feel you ought to do this year
   ______
5. something you'd rather do now instead of homework
   ______
6. three things you're going to have to do tomorrow
   ______

Lesson C I've got to get going.

1 I can't talk right now.

Conversation strategies

Ming-li and Ivana want to make plans, but they always call each other at the wrong time. Complete the expressions they use to end their conversations.

2 Talk to you later!

Conversation strategies

Circle the best response. Then write the shorter form.

1. A Oh, hi. Can I call you back later?
   B *Sure. Talk to you later.*
   a. Sure. I'd better go.
   (b.) Sure. I'll talk to you later.

2. A I'm really sorry. I've got to go out in two minutes.
   B ______________________
   a. No problem. I've got to go, too. Bye.
   b. No problem. I'm not busy.

3. A Let's talk tomorrow.
   B ______________________
   a. OK. Now's a good time.
   b. OK. I'll catch you later.

4. A Well, anyway, I'd better go.
   B ______________________
   a. OK. I'll see you later.
   b. OK. I can't talk right now.

5. A I'm so glad you called. It was fun to catch up.
   B ______________________
   a. Yeah, I'll call you later.
   b. Yeah, it was nice talking to you, too!

6. A I'd better go. I'm late.
   B ______________________
   a. That's OK. I'm free now.
   b. That's OK. I'd better go, too.

3 The end?

Conversation strategies

Imagine you're trying to leave your house to go to your English class, but four friends call you. Try to end each conversation. Then use a "friendly" good-bye.

1. Liliana Hi, it's me. Listen, I have a problem. Do you have some time to talk?
   You *Not really. I've got to go to English class. Can I call you back?*
   Liliana OK.
   You *Talk to you later.*

2. Hans Hi, it's Hans. Are you busy right now? I need to ask you a question.
   You ______________________
   Hans No problem.
   You ______________________

3. Doug Hey! Guess what? I have some exciting news for you!
   You ______________________
   Doug Fine. Call me when you get home later.
   You ______________________

4. Louisa Hi! It's Louisa. I didn't understand the homework. Did you?
   You ______________________
   Louisa All right. Well, maybe we can meet in the library tomorrow.
   You ______________________

1 Getting organized

Reading **A Read the article. Then add the correct heading to each section.**

Save money Save space Save time

Tips that $ave

Whether your schedule is crazy, your apartment is cluttered, or your budget is mismanaged, here are some tips to get more organized.

[ ]

Do you find it difficult to find really good birthday presents because you wait until the last minute? And then do you spend hours in the stores because you can't find anything you like?

Whenever you're shopping and you see a gift at a great price, buy it and put it in your closet. When a special occasion comes up and you need a gift for someone, you'll have a selection of things to choose from. You won't have to make a special trip for last-minute shopping.

Do you ever pay bills late because you lose them in all the papers and clutter in your home? Well, if you need a system for paying your bills on time, the trick is to pay them online. You can arrange to pay your bills directly from your bank account. Once you have set up online bill pay, you can either set up a reminder for yourself to pay on a certain date, or you can have your bills paid automatically.

[ ]

Magazines can take over your home before you know it. Most magazines are also available online. Save space by reading the articles online. Or, if you like to read a print magazine and want to save an article, go online and download the article to your computer. Then read it again whenever you want.

Buy brightly colored baskets or boxes for your shelves to store smaller items neatly. Label them with their contents. Your shelves will look neater, and you'll have more space for your larger items. Hang single shelves above doorways to store things you rarely use. Place low shelves in your closet to take advantage of unused space.

[ ]

Save for a rainy day, little by little. It's easy to make progress if you give yourself a weekly allowance. Try to spend less than your allowance each week. Put the remaining money in an envelope. At the end of each month, put the money in your bank account.

It's the little habits that count. Have you added up the cost of those cappuccinos you buy every morning? If you spend $3.50 on coffee five days a week, that adds up to $910 a year! By doing without fancy drinks and making your coffee at home, you can save a bundle. You might want to try packing a lunch instead of eating at the local café, too – this habit can also save you hundreds a year.

B Find these words and expressions in the article. Match them with the definitions.

1. clutter __e__
2. the trick ____
3. take advantage of ____
4. a rainy day ____
5. count ____
6. doing without ____
7. a bundle ____

a. make use of
b. a time when you need money
c. not having
d. a lot of money
e. mess
f. make a difference
g. best thing to do

C Read the article again. Then write *T* (true), *F* (false), or *D* (doesn't say).

1. __T__ Buy gifts cheaply when you see them; you can decide who they're for later.
2. _____ You can save money if you pay your bills late.
3. _____ Downloading articles to your computer is a good way to save time.
4. _____ You can save space on your shelves if you put lots of small things into boxes.
5. _____ It's better to keep your money in an envelope than a bank.
6. _____ You should make more food at home.

2 Making room

Writing

A Read the article. Add *as long as*, *provided that*, and *unless* to link ideas. Sometimes more than one answer is possible.

Your closet is overflowing, and you need to make room for new clothes. How do you decide what to do with all your old clothes? First, get a box and put in everything you hardly ever wear, ______________ they aren't clothes for special occasions.

Give them all to a charity store ______________ you have some valuable clothes you can sell. Next, use the "two-season rule." Separate your remaining clothes by season. If it's winter, put your winter clothes back in the closet. Buy some under-the-bed boxes for your off-season clothes. If it's summer, store all your sweaters under your bed, ______________ the space under your bed isn't already cluttered!

B Write a short article giving advice about how to reduce clutter, save money, or save time. Try to use *as long as*, *provided that*, and *unless* to link ideas.

Unit 6 Progress chart

	What can you do? Mark the boxes. ✓ = I can . . . ? = I need to review how to . . .	To review, go back to these pages in the Student's Book.
Grammar	☐ talk about the future using *will*, *going to*, the present continuous, and the simple present.	54 and 55
	☐ use *ought to*, *have got to*, *would rather*, *had better*, etc.	56 and 57
Vocabulary	☐ use at least 12 expressions with *do* or *make*.	56
Conversation strategies	☐ use at least 5 different expressions to end a phone conversation.	58
	☐ say good-bye in an informal, friendly way.	59
Writing	☐ use *as long as*, *provided that*, and *unless* to link ideas.	61

Relationships

UNIT 7

Lesson A / Circle of friends

1 He's the guy . . .

Grammar **Choose the correct relative pronoun to complete each sentence. If a relative pronoun is not needed, circle the dash (–).**

1. This is Andrew. He's the guy **which** / – I met on vacation in Florida.

2. This is the dog **that** / **who** followed me on the beach one day. It turned out to be Andrew's dog. So I guess it was the dog **that** / – introduced us.

3. This is the amusement park **who** / – we went to on our first date. And this is the ticket for the first movie **that** / **who** we saw.

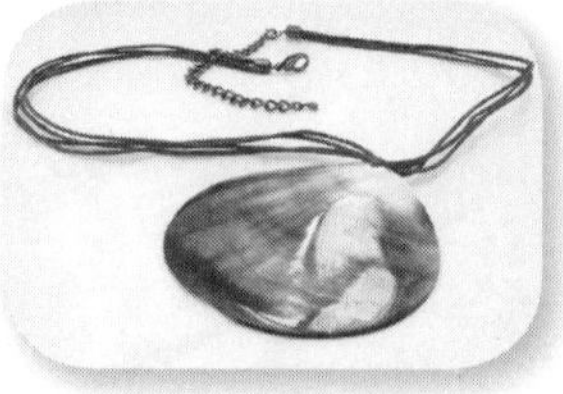

4. Here's the necklace **that** / **who** he gave me before I left for home. Andrew is someone **which** / **who** I'm going to keep in touch with.

5. This is the letter **that** / – came three days after I got back. Inside is the photo **who** / – he took of me the day I left.

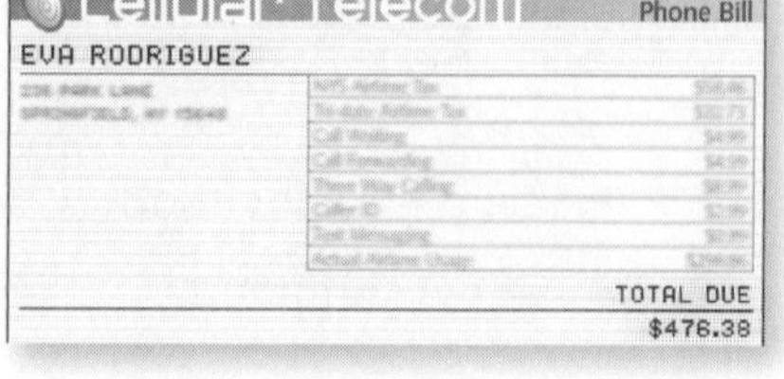

6. We talk every day. And this is the phone bill **who** / **that** I got yesterday!

2 She's the girl . . .

Grammar | **Complete the email with *who*, *that*, or *which*. Put the word in parentheses ( ) if the sentence is also complete without the relative pronoun. Sometimes more than one answer is possible.**

New Message

To: mel_bes@cup.com
From: camilleS@cup.com
Subject: Estella and Ramiro

Dear Melania,

I'm so excited about some news *(that / which)* I just got from a friend. You know Estella, right? She's my friend from Peru ______ I met in college. Well, last year I introduced her to that cute guy, Ramiro, ______ I used to work with. He had the desk ______ was across from mine. Anyway, a group of us used to go out together sometimes after work. One day, I invited Estella along. (I knew Ramiro was exactly the kind of guy ______ she would like.) We went to the Caribbean restaurant ______ I love on Essex Street. To make a long story short, they met that night, and now they're getting married. I just got the invitation. I can't wait for the wedding!

Camille

3 I have a friend . . .

Grammar | **Use the sentences in the box and *who*, *that*, or *which* to complete the sentences below. Put the relative pronoun in parentheses ( ) if the sentence is also complete without it. Sometimes more than one answer is possible.**

Her family owns a store.	It served traditional Korean food.	The paper has rose petals in it.
I spoke to her in Korean.	✓She lives in South Korea.	The shop sells handmade paper.

1. I have a friend, Seung-Li, *who / that lives in South Korea* .
2. I met her in Seoul at the store ______ .
3. It is a very special shop ______ .
4. I bought some paper ______ .
5. She was the only person ______ .
6. Later, she invited me to a restaurant ______ .

4 About you

Grammar | **Complete the sentences with true information. Use relative pronouns where necessary.**

1. I have a friend *who speaks three languages* .
2. My neighbor is someone ______ .
3. I like stores ______ .
4. I take a class ______ .
5. I don't like the food ______ .
6. I know someone ______ .

1 Which particle?

Grammar and vocabulary

Circle the correct particle to complete each sentence.

1. My sister's not home. She went **up** / **away** / **along** for the weekend.
2. I grew **out** / **down** / **up** in Morocco, but now I live in California.
3. My brother isn't ready to settle **out** / **up** / **down**. He doesn't want to get married yet.
4. My mother's away on business now, but she plans to fly **away** / **along** / **back** next Tuesday.
5. I thought I had a doctor's appointment today, but it turns **out** / **up** / **down** that it's next week.
6. My best friend is moving **up** / **away** / **along** next month. I'm going to miss her.
7. I forgot to sign **back** / **out** / **up** for the class trip to the museum, so I can't go.
8. I sent my cousin an email last week, but he never wrote **back** / **away** / **out**.

2 Figure it out!

Grammar and vocabulary

Complete the sentences with the phrasal verbs in the box. Then complete the puzzle and the sentence below.

come back	go away	sign up	✓write back
get along	grow up	work out	

1. When a friend sends you an email, you should _write back_ immediately.
2. If a relationship doesn't ____________, don't worry about it. It may be for the best.
3. If you want to ____________ well with someone, be a good friend!
4. It's good to take a break from your usual routine and ____________ for a few days.
5. It's fun to go on vacation, but it's always good to ____________ home, too!
6. A lot of kids ____________ in blended families these days.
7. One way to meet new people is to ____________ for a class.

1. w r i t e [b] a c k
2. _ _ [ ] _   _ _ _
3. _ [ ] _   _ _ _ _ _
4. _ _ [ ] _ _ _
5. _ _ _ _   _ _ _ [ ]
6. _ _ _ _ [ ] _
7. _ _ _ _   _ [ ]

Some couples like to ____________ ____________ because they think it's fun to make up and get back together!

3 Breaking up is hard to do.

Grammar and vocabulary

Complete the conversation with the correct form of the phrasal verbs in the box. Sometimes more than one answer is possible.

✓break up	go out	turn out
get along	hang out	work out

Tina Hi, Jorge. You don't look so good. What's wrong?

Jorge Well, my girlfriend and I *broke up* last week.

Tina Oh, no. You did? That's too bad. How long were you ____________ with her?

Jorge About three months. I can't believe things didn't ____________. I mean, we ____________ really well. I thought everything was fine.

Tina Yeah, you guys were always ____________ together.

Jorge I know. We saw each other almost every day!

Tina Well, maybe that was the problem. Maybe she didn't want to spend every minute of every day with you.

Jorge Yeah, I guess you're right. Things didn't ____________ the way I thought.

Tina Why don't you talk to her? Ask her what she wants in a relationship.

4 About you

Grammar and vocabulary

Answer the questions with true information.

1. Who do you get along well with? Why?
   I get along well with my sister because we are very similar.
2. Do you like to go away for summer vacation?
   ____
3. Where do you and your friends like to hang out?
   ____
4. Do you always write back immediately when someone sends you an email?
   ____
5. Are there any classes you would like to sign up for?
   ____
6. Do you think you'll ever move far away from home?
   ____

1 I guess . . .

Conversation strategies | **Rewrite each sentence with the two "softening" expressions in parentheses to complete the conversations.**

1. A What's wrong with Jamil? He just yelled at me for turning on the TV.

   B *He's probably just tired.* He stayed
   He's tired. (probably / just)
   up all night. He had to finish a paper for school.

   A He always waits until the last minute to do his work.

   B I know. ____________________
   He's disorganized. (I guess / kind of)

   A Yeah, and he has so many activities at school.
   ____
   He's doing too much. (I think / a bit)

   B But it's good to be involved with your school.

   A That's true. ____________________
   He's stressed out. (I guess / sort of)

2. A Have you met Alissa yet? She's the new student in our class.

   B Yeah. I talked to her yesterday, but she didn't say much.

   A ____________________
   She's shy. (maybe / just)

   B Yeah, I'm sure she'll meet people soon.
   ____
   It takes time. (just / a little)

   A It's difficult when you don't know anyone.

   B I know. ____________________
   It's hard to fit in. (I think / sort of)

   A Yeah. ____________________
   Making friends is hard. (I guess / in a way)

2 It's spicy, though.

Conversation strategies

Complete the conversations with the responses in the box. Add *though* if appropriate.

He's pretty shy.	I'll find out when he's free.
He's here for two weeks.	It was a little spicy.
✓ I love Thai food.	It was really nice.

1. **Lee** How was your dinner date last night?
   Kyra Great. We went to a Thai restaurant that Wayne knows.
   Lee Cool. *I love Thai food.* What did you have?
   Kyra Green curry with chicken and a vegetable dish.
   Lee Was it good?
   Kyra Yeah, the food was excellent. ________________ I don't usually like spicy food, but I really enjoyed it.
   Lee Was it expensive?
   Kyra Well, it was a little expensive. ________________

2. **Becky** Brad, who's the new guy in your department?
   Brad Oh, that's Bart. He's just visiting from the Los Angeles office. ________________
   Becky Only two weeks? That's too bad. He seems interesting.
   Brad Yeah. ________________ He's probably kind of lonely.
   Becky Well, maybe we should invite him to dinner. Then we could show him around a little before he leaves.
   Brad That sounds like a great idea. ________________

3 About you

Conversation strategies

Use true information to answer each set of questions. Respond to the first question using "softening" comments. Then respond to the second question using *though*.

1. What's something you're bad at? What's something you're good at?
   I guess I'm kind of bad at playing tennis. I'm really great at playing chess, though.
2. What's your worst quality? What's your best quality?
   ____
3. What's difficult about learning English? What do you like about learning English?
   ____
4. What annoying habit does one of your friends have? What's nice about him or her?
   ____
5. What's your least favorite kind of music? What's your favorite kind?
   ____

Lesson D New friends, old friends

1 Interactive communities

Reading **A Read the article. What topics are discussed? Check (✓) all that apply.**

☐ dating sites ☐ meeting people offline ☐ phone apps ☐ social networking

Using the online world to go offline

With our ability to connect to almost anyone in the world at any time, are we feeling more alone than ever? That's the question that critics of technology are asking. Some research suggests that people who use the Internet and social networks a lot often feel isolated and lonelier than people who don't. Supporters of online socializing disagree and point out that it's up to the user whether or not an online relationship becomes a meaningful, face-to-face one. After all, social networks, Internet companies, and app developers are merely doing their job – connecting users online. The next steps from online to offline are for us, the users, to take.

In fact, social networking websites often give us all the tools we need to move easily from an online relationship to an offline one. For example, there are websites that organize groups around particular interests. Perhaps you've just moved to a new city and want to meet people who have the same interests as you. You can sign up on websites that help you find others who enjoy the same hobbies. Many of these groups plan face-to-face activities. It's a great way to connect with people you would never meet otherwise. There's no guarantee that you'll get along, but at least you'll have something in common.

Apps for cell phones or tablets can also help us connect with people offline in several ways. Some apps let you find friends nearby, find out what they are doing, and who's available to hang out. Other apps help you plan activities. You can send an invitation to friends electronically and include details about the activity, maps, and directions for how to get there. The people you invite can respond in the same way. There are also apps that recommend where you can meet people, for example, at restaurants or museums.

Technology doesn't have to isolate us. There are plenty of websites and phone apps that help us create social networks, both online and in real life. The trick is to make the effort. At some point, we have to pull our attention away from the screen in order to actually meet someone.

B Read the article again. Are the sentences true, false, or is the information not given? Write *T* (true), *F* (false), or *D* (doesn't say).

1. People who spend too much time online can feel lonely. <u>T</u>
2. The writer suggests that social networks are to blame for people's loneliness. ____
3. Websites that are for people with similar interests connect people that get along. ____
4. If you sign up for a website that organizes face-to-face activities, you'll meet new people that you like. ____
5. Most people only want to use websites and apps to find dates, not to find friends. ____
6. Technology can improve your relationships with your circle of friends. ____

2 Common ground

Writing

A Read the email. Then complete the sentences with *both*, *both of us*, or *neither of us*.

New Message

To: mitch_88@cup.com
From: PhilJ@cup.com
Subject: Your high school friend

Dear Mitch,

Remember me from high school? I'm the guy who sat behind you in world literature class. I got your email address from Kurt, the guy we *both* used to hang out with at lunchtime.

I'll always remember that class. ____________ hated reading those short stories, but we had to take the class for some reason. And ____________ liked our teacher, Mr. What's-his-name. He wasn't a very good teacher at all. It's amazing that we ____________ passed the final exam. Good thing we ____________ stayed up late studying the night before.

Anyway, I was talking to Kurt last week, and ____________ would like to see you again. Maybe we can all meet and go out for dinner or something one day soon.

Take care,
Phil

B Write an email to an old friend you haven't seen in a long time. Include things you did and didn't have in common.

New Message

To: buddy1@cup.com
From: buddy2@cup.com
Subject: Long time no see!

____

____

____

____

Unit 7 Progress chart

	What can you do? Mark the boxes. ✓ = I can . . . ? = I need to review how to . . .	To review, go back to these pages in the Student's Book.
Grammar	☐ write sentences with subject and object relative clauses. ☐ use phrasal verbs like *grow up*, *get along*, and *break up*.	66 and 67 68 and 69
Vocabulary	☐ use at least 12 phrasal verbs.	68 and 69
Conversation strategies	☐ use at least 6 expressions to soften comments. ☐ give a contrasting idea using *though*.	70 71
Writing	☐ use *both*, *both of us*, and *neither of us*.	73

What if?

UNIT 8

Lesson A Wishes

1 When you wish . . .

Grammar **A** What are these people wishing for right now? Complete the sentences.

1. James *wishes he had a new car* .

2. Emi and Sue ______________________ .

3. Joey ______________________ .

4. Esteban and Pilar ______________________ .

5. Al ______________________ .

6. Li-ming ______________________ .

B **Complete the sentences about the people in part A.**

1. If James *had* (have) more money, he *would buy* (buy) a new car.
2. If Emi and Sue ________ (live) in a bigger apartment, they ____________ (have) more space.
3. If Joey ________ (be) taller, he ____________ (score) more points.
4. If Esteban and Pilar ________ (have) two TVs, they ____________ (not have) to watch the same TV shows.
5. If Al ________ (not be) a bad cook, he ____________ (eat) better.
6. If Li-ming ________ (live) in the country, she ____________ (be) much happier.

2 About you

Grammar | **Write true sentences about your wishes.**

My Wish List

1. I wish I *had more free time during the week* . (have)
   If I *had more free time during the week, I'd exercise more* . (have)
2. I wish I ____________________ . (be)
   If I ____________________ . (be)
3. I wish I ____________________ . (can)
   If I ____________________ . (can)
4. I wish I ____________________ . (not be)
   If I ____________________ . (not be)
5. I wish my parents ____________________ . (not be)
   If they ____________________ . (not be)
6. I wish my friend ____________________ . (be)
   If he or she ____________________ . (be)
7. I wish I ____________________ . (have)
   If I ____________________ . (have)
8. I wish I ____________________ . (not have to)
   If I ____________________ . (not have to)
9. I wish I ____________________ . (live)
   If I ____________________ . (live)

1 If I had a problem, . . .

Vocabulary | **Circle the correct word to complete each sentence. Then decide if each sentence is true or false for you. Write *T* (true) or *F* (false). Correct the false statements.**

1. _F_ If I had a problem, I would talk **for** / **(to)** / **about** my best friend.
   If I had a problem, I would talk to my Aunt Lisa.
2. ____ I always apologize **about** / **to** / **for** my mistakes.
   ____
3. ____ My friends never thank me **for** / **about** / **with** helping them.
   ____
4. ____ I always worry **for** / **about** / **from** taking tests!
   ____
5. ____ I often share books **to** / **with** / **about** my neighbors.
   ____
6. ____ If I forgot **with** / **from** / **about** a friend's birthday, I would feel bad.
   ____

2 Remind me about it.

Vocabulary | **Complete the conversations with the words in the box.**

ask for	✓forget about	remind about	worry about
borrow from	lend to	talk to	
buy for	pay for	think about	

1. A Where's Marissa? I hope she didn't _forget_ _about_ our party.
   B I know. Let's call her and ________ her ________ it.
2. A Oh, no. I forgot my wallet. Can I ________ some money ________ you for lunch?
   B Oh, don't ________ ________ it. I'll get lunch. It's my treat!
3. A Do you think I should ________ this camera ________ my sister's birthday?
   B Why don't you ________ ________ her about it first?
4. A Can you ________ ten dollars ________ Lenny to buy a movie ticket?
   B I'm sorry. I can't. I have just enough to ________ ________ my own ticket.
5. A I think we're lost. Should we ________ someone ________ directions to the museum?
   B Not yet. I'm sure if I ________ ________ it for a minute, I'll remember how to get there.

3 Would you ask for an autograph?

Grammar | **Complete the questions with the correct form of the verbs.**

1. What *would you say* (say) if you *met* (meet) a famous athlete? *Would you ask* (ask) for an autograph?
2. If you ______ (see) an accident, what ______ (do)? ______ (call) for an ambulance?
3. What ______ (do) if you ______ (have) a large spider on your leg? ______ (scream)?
4. If you ______ (break) your best friend's camera, how ______ (feel)? ______ (offer) to replace it?
5. How ______ (react) if your best friend ______ (win) a trip to Hawai'i? ______ (feel) jealous?
6. What ______ (say) to your neighbors if they ______ (complain) about your music? ______ (apologize)?

4 About you

Grammar | **Answer the questions in Exercise 3. Write true information.**

1. *If I met a famous athlete, I'd say, "I really admire you!" I would definitely ask for an autograph.*

2. ______
3. ______
4. ______
5. ______
6. ______

Lesson C / If I were you, . . .

1 I'd choose . . .

Conversation strategies

Complete the conversation with the expressions in the box. Sometimes more than one answer is possible.

✓if I were you, I'd	I would	I wouldn't	you could	you might want to

Serge I really want to take a vacation this summer, but I need to work, too.

Nina Well, *if I were you, I'd* take a vacation first. You might not get another chance.

Serge Hmm. Maybe I should. Where's a good place to go – any ideas?

Nina Well, there are so many great places. I mean, ____________ go anywhere. Have you been to Europe?

Serge No. I'd love to. It's kind of expensive, though.

Nina Well, ____________ let that stop you! Seriously, you can always get a job there. There are programs for students who want to work abroad. ____________ find out about them if I were you.

Serge I never thought of that.

Nina ____________ look on the Internet and do a little research.

Serge Yeah. That's a great idea. So, I could work *and* take a vacation.

2 Good advice

Conversation strategies

Grace is having a bad day. Respond to her statements with advice.

1. Grace I didn't do very well on my math exam.
   You *If I were you, I'd talk to the teacher.*
2. Grace Ouch! I just got a bad paper cut.
   You ____________________________
3. Grace Oh, no! My car won't start.
   You ____________________________
4. Grace I just stained my favorite sweater.
   You ____________________________

3 You might want to . . .

Conversation strategies | **Look at the pictures. Complete the advice.**

1. You look tired. *I would get some coffee*.

2. The sun's really strong. I ______________________.

3. It's very windy. If ______________________.

4. It's very cold. You ______________________.

4 That would be fun.

Conversation strategies | **Respond to each sentence with *That would be* and an appropriate adjective.**

1. I'd really like to hike in the Himalayas. — *Wow. That would be awesome!*
2. Maybe we could go to the mall this afternoon. — ______________________
3. It would be great to win a million dollars. — ______________________
4. One day, I'm going to learn to tango. — ______________________

1 What do you regret?

Reading | **A Read the article about regrets. According to the article, which of the following factors affect how people regret things in life?**

☐ age ☐ climate ☐ culture ☐ gender ☐ health ☐ income

Regrets? Too few to mention

Do you ever lie awake at night with regrets? Do you spend hours wishing you could change your life? __5__ If so, you're not alone. Regret – that negative feeling you have after a bad experience – is a fairly common human emotion. However, recent research suggests that while almost everyone experiences regret at some point or another, it is much more negative for some than for others.

What do we regret? According to research, we tend to regret decisions we made about our education, careers, romance, and parenting. We feel bad about things we did. ____ We wish we had different life opportunities, could make different choices, and relive moments with different outcomes. However, the nature and impact of regrets can vary across ages, sex, and cultures.

From the research, it would seem that the most striking difference in how regret affects people is between younger and older people. Younger people tend to regret the things they actually did, whereas older people regret the things they didn't do – their missed opportunities. Older people experience regret much more negatively. ____ Younger people are more likely to see a bad experience as an important learning opportunity. They realize they made a mistake, and they use that to guide their decisions in the future. Older people don't feel they have the same chance to correct their actions and their outcomes.

Gender and culture can also affect what and how we regret. ____ According to some research, more women may regret lost romantic opportunities and family conflicts. More men may regret their decisions around career, money, and education. In cultures that put a high value on personal choice, such as the United States, people tend to have more regrets. In cultures where the family or the community makes more decisions, people have fewer regrets. Research suggests that the more choices we have, the more possibilities we have to regret.

So, if you find yourself staring at the ceiling at 3 a.m., what can you do to turn your regret into something positive? Use it to make better choices in the future. Realize that you couldn't control everything in the past situation. Take more chances in the future. ____ And be a little easier on yourself.

B Read the article again. Then add these missing sentences to the article by writing each number in the correct blank.

1. The differences between men and women are interesting.
2. We may feel worse about the things we didn't do.
3. Have more fun.
4. It can even lead to depression in some older people.
5. Do you torture yourself thinking about your mistakes?

C Choose the correct options to complete the sentences.

1. Feeling regret is **not common** / **normal**.
2. The feeling of regret is **worse for some** / **the same for everyone**.
3. Older people mostly regret things they **did** / **didn't do**.
4. **Younger** / **Older** people feel they are in a better position to avoid the same mistakes.
5. Regret is **more** / **less** common when people make their own decisions.
6. The article suggests that in the end, regret is **useless** / **useful**.

2 If I won the lottery, . . .

Writing **A** Read the journal entry. Complete the sentences with the adverbs given and the correct verb forms.

If I won the lottery, I 'd definitely quit ____________ (definitely / quit) my job, and I ____________ (probably / not work) at all! If I were a millionaire, I ____________ (definitely / buy) a house on the beach and one in the mountains. If I had two houses, I ____________ (definitely / invite) my family and friends to visit, but I ____________ (probably / not invite) them every weekend. I'd want some time for myself. If I had more time for myself, I'd write more, and I ____________ (probably / try) to publish a book. What would the title of the book be? "How to Live Like a Millionaire," of course!

B Write a journal entry about what you would do if you were a millionaire. Use *definitely* and *probably* to show degrees of certainty.

____

____

____

Unit 8 Progress chart

	What can you do? Mark the boxes. ✓ = I can . . . ? = I need to review how to . . .	To review, go back to these pages in the Student's Book.
Grammar	☐ use *wish* + past form of verb for wishes about the present or future.	76 and 77
	☐ use *If* + past form of verb, followed by *would* / *could* + verb to talk about imaginary situations in the present or future.	76, 77, and 79
Vocabulary	☐ use the correct preposition after at least 12 verbs.	78
Conversation strategies	☐ give advice using expressions like *If I were you* and *You could*.	80
	☐ use *That would be* to comment on a possibility or a suggestion.	81
Writing	☐ use *definitely* and *probably* to show degrees of certainty.	83

Tech savvy?

UNIT 9

Lesson A Tech support

1 I have no idea why . . .

Grammar **A Unscramble the questions.**

1. which battery / Do you know / should / buy / I / ?
   Do you know which battery I should buy?
2. they / where / are / Can you tell me / ?
   ____
3. when / you / Can you remember / it / last changed / ?
   ____
4. it / Do you have any idea / how much / costs / ?
   ____

B Unscramble the statements.

1. why / isn't / I have no idea / working / it
   ____
2. last changed it / when / I don't know / I
   ____
3. two / I / if / I wonder / should / batteries / buy
   ____

C Complete the conversation with the questions and statements from parts A and B.

Woman Excuse me. Can you help me?
Clerk Sure. What seems to be the problem?
Woman It's my camera. *I have no idea why it isn't working.*
Clerk Hmm. Let me look at it. It might be the battery. ______________________
Woman No, I can't. ______________________ I'm not sure if I've ever changed it.
Clerk Well, you definitely need a new one.
Woman ______________________
Clerk You need a 3.7 volt battery.
Woman ______________________
Clerk They're $39.99 each.
Woman Great. ______________________
Clerk Sure. They're at the back of the store. Here, let me show you.
Woman Thanks. ______________________ Maybe I should have an extra one.
Clerk That might be a good idea.

2 I wonder . . .

Grammar | **A Tara wants to download some music from the Internet. Rewrite the questions she wants to ask her friend Kwang.**

1. Can you download songs from this website?
2. How do you put them on your phone?
3. Is there a charge for each song?
4. Can you buy just one song?
5. How do you pay for the songs?
6. How do you make a playlist?
7. Are there any free songs?
8. Can I put the songs on my tablet, too?

1. I wonder *if you can download songs from this website* ________.
2. Can you tell me ________________?
3. Do you know ________________?
4. Do you have any idea ________________?
5. Do you know ________________?
6. Can you remember ________________?
7. I wonder ________________.
8. Do you know ________________?

B Kwang doesn't know the answers to Tara's questions. Write his replies using the expressions in the box. Use each expression twice.

I don't know	I can't remember	I have no idea	I'm not sure

1. *I don't know if you can download songs from this website.*
2. ________________
3. ________________
4. ________________
5. ________________
6. ________________
7. ________________
8. ________________

Lesson B How things work

1 You should put it down.

Grammar and vocabulary **Complete the sentences with the phrasal verbs in the box. Add the correct pronouns.**

look up	put away	put on	take apart	throw away
print out	✓put down	set up	take off	turn off

1. Thanks for bringing in the box of groceries. Could you *put it down* over here?
2. I did something awful to my computer. I tried to __________ , and now I can't get all the pieces back in it.
3. I hate those sticky price labels on things you buy. I can never __________ .
4. My game controller doesn't work anymore. I wonder if I should just __________ .
5. There's nothing good on TV. Do you mind if I __________ ?
6. I just bought these new headphones. Do you want to __________ and try them out?
7. I downloaded a video-chat app, but I can't __________ .
8. I don't know what this word means. Maybe I should __________ on the Internet.
9. My brother leaves his video games all over the floor. He should __________ , or they'll get damaged.
10. After you write documents, do you __________ to read them?

2 Step-by-step

Grammar and vocabulary **Complete the conversation with the words in the box.**

hook up / the computer	✓turn down / the air conditioning
pick up / the monitor	turn on / the radio
plug in / all the cables	turn up / the volume

Ruth We found this great apartment, but it's so cold in here.

Kate Oh, I'll *turn down the air conditioning* .
There we go. So, what do you want to do first?

Ruth Let's put some music on.
Can you ____________________ ?

Kate Sure. Is that loud enough?

Ruth Not really. Can you ____________________ ? Thanks.

Kate I'd like to ____________________ , so I can check my email.

Ruth OK, let's put the computer over by the window.
I'll ____________________ .
You get the computer and the cables.

Kate OK. You know, I have no idea where to ____________________ .

Ruth I'm sure we can figure it out. Do you know where the manual is?

3 What to do?

Grammar and vocabulary | **Complete the conversations using the given words. Write A's suggestions in two different ways. Then use the correct pronoun in B's response.**

1. A Before you go out, *put on your hat and gloves*.
   Before you go out, *put your hat and gloves on*.
   (put on / your hat and gloves)
   B If I get too warm, can I *take them off* ________ ?
   (take off)

2. A ________________ in a dictionary.
   ________________ in a dictionary.
   (look up / the new words)
   B Can we ________________ on the Internet?
   (look up)

3. A You have to ________________ gently.
   You have to ________________ gently.
   (put in / the DVD)
   B If it doesn't work, should I ________________ ?
   (take out)

4. A The kitchen's so messy. We should ________________ .
   The kitchen's so messy. We should ________________ .
   (put away / the dishes)
   B Actually, why don't we ________________ ?
   (throw away)

4 About you

Grammar | **Complete the questions. Then fill in the survey with true answers.**

	Yes	No
1. Can you explain to someone *how to set up voice mail on a phone* ? (how / set up voice mail on a phone)	☐	☐
2. Do you have any idea ________________ on your computer? (where / plug in the headphones)	☐	☐
3. Could you tell someone ________________ ? (how / use your TV remote)	☐	☐
4. Do you know ________________ on the Internet? (how / look up information)	☐	☐
5. Do you have any idea ________________ when your computer crashes? (what / do)	☐	☐
6. Do you know ________________ on your computer? (how / change the password)	☐	☐

1 Don't you think . . . ?

Conversation strategies

A Match Cameron's opinions with her friends' responses.

1. I think kids watch too much TV. _f_
2. I think video games are totally boring and stupid. ____
3. I don't think people should drive big cars. ____
4. It's a shame no one writes letters anymore. I used to love getting them. ____
5. Kids need to spend less time on the computer. ____
6. I don't like shopping on the Internet. You can't see what you're buying. ____

a. I know what you mean, but with email, you can get in touch with people more often and faster.
b. I'm not so sure. Don't you think they can learn a lot online, too? I mean, there are some good educational websites.
c. Maybe. People with large families need to have big cars, though.
d. I don't know. I find it saves me time because I don't have to go to the store and wait in line.
e. I know what you mean, but there are so many different kinds of games. You could probably find something you liked.
f. That's true. On the other hand, kids need to relax sometimes, and we all have our favorite shows.

B Write your own responses to Cameron's opinions in part A. Use the expressions in the box if you disagree with her.

I know what you mean, but . . .	I don't know.
I'm not (so) sure. Don't you think . . . ?	✓That's true. . . . , though.
Maybe.	On the other hand, . . .

1. _That's true. I think some TV shows are educational, though._
2. ______________________________
3. ______________________________
4. ______________________________
5. ______________________________
6. ______________________________

2 What's your opinion?

Conversation strategies

Write opinions about the topics. Then add an expression from the box to get someone to agree with you. Use each expression twice.

You know what I mean?	You know?	You know what I'm saying?

1. Texting is *really convenient. But it's really annoying when you're trying to have a conversation with someone who's texting at the same time. You know what I mean?*
2. Video calling is ______________________________
3. Blogging is ______________________________
4. Online video clips are ______________________________
5. Tablets are ______________________________
6. Social networking is ______________________________

3 I don't know.

Conversation strategies

Respond to each statement with a different opinion. Try to convince the other person to agree with you.

1. Kids spend too much time on the Internet.

   I don't know. I think it's great they learn how to use computers when they're so young. You know?

2. Teens shouldn't go to school and work at the same time. It's too hard.

   ____

3. I think too many people are addicted to their computers and phones and everything.

   ____

4. You never know if things you see on the Internet are true.

   ____

1 Spam-a-lot

Reading **A Read the article. Then check (✓) the best title.**

☐ How to Be a Successful Spammer
☐ Where to Send Spam
☐ How Companies Avoid Spam
☐ Don't Be a Victim – How You Can Avoid Spam

Are you fed up with junk email and spam that fills up your inbox every day? Spam isn't just annoying for home users of computers. It's becoming a serious problem for businesses, too. Getting rid of spam wastes employees' time. Spam takes up space on computers, and it can slow down – or even jam – normal email traffic.

Most people don't know how spammers get their email address, but in fact, it's very easy. Your email address may be on any number of Internet sites such as blogs, email newsletters, company directories, and many other lists on the Web. You can also become a spam victim if you've entered an online contest or responded to a survey using your email address.

Spammers also use software that generates email addresses automatically. This software makes up millions of email addresses by using common names and the addresses of well-known companies and Internet service providers. It then sends out messages to all the addresses it creates. Although some of them might not work and the messages "bounce back," many others will get through to real people. The spammers now have a valuable list of valid addresses, which they can sell to other spammers at high prices.

HOW TO PROTECT YOURSELF FROM SPAM

DO:

- Change your email address regularly. Create an address that is difficult to guess. For example, if your name is Kevin Smith and you love cycling, try an address like KSmith4biking@cup.org. Or if you live in Toronto, you could use KS_in_Toronto@cup.org.
- Have two email addresses – one for public use and a private one only for friends and family.
- Buy anti-spam software or use email filters. Many email programs have filters that automatically send spam to a junk-mail folder. Be sure to check the junk-mail folder periodically for any personal mail that goes there by mistake.
- Pay attention to typos and misspellings in email subject lines. These are warning signs of possible spam.

DON'T:

- Respond to spam – ever. When you respond, you confirm that your address is valid.
- Buy anything from a company that sent you spam. This supports their belief that spamming makes money.

B Find the underlined words in the article. Then circle the best meaning.

1. Spam can jam normal email traffic.	a. slow down	(b.) stop or block
2. You can become a spam victim.	a. someone who gets spam	b. someone who sends spam
3. The software generates addresses.	a. creates	b. gets rid of
4. Some messages "bounce back."	a. get to the people	b. go back to the spammers
5. They have a list of valid addresses.	a. real	b. false
6. Never confirm your address.	a. forget	b. say it's correct

2 Get rid of it!

Writing | **A Read the list of ideas, and add an idea of your own. Then use the ideas to complete the article.**

Ways to prevent spam

- Get another email address. Use one email address for chat rooms and message boards.
- Tell friends and family how to prevent spam.
- Use spam-filtering software.
- Don't respond to spam.
- ______________________

How to get rid of spam

First of all, keep your personal email address private. If you want to participate in chat rooms or on *message boards*, get a second ______________ from a free email provider. Second, don't ______________ to spam, even when it provides a link to "unsubscribe" from the list. Spammers see that your address is valid and sell it to other spammers. Third, use the ______________ on your computer. Fourth, ______________________. Finally, tell ______________ about these tips. If fewer people respond to spam, there will be less spam!

B Brainstorm ideas on one of these topics. Then plan and write a short article.

- How to avoid identity theft
- How to protect yourself from theft
- How to use the Internet safely
- How to get help with computer problems

Ideas

____

Unit 9 Progress chart

What can you do? Mark the boxes. ✓ = I can . . . ? = I need to review how to . . .	To review, go back to these pages in the Student's Book.
Grammar	
☐ use questions within questions and statements.	86 and 87
☐ use *how to*, *where to*, and *what to* + verb.	88
☐ use separable phrasal verbs like *turn on* and *plug in*.	88
Vocabulary	
☐ use at least 12 phrasal verbs.	88 and 89
Conversation strategies	
☐ use expressions to give a different opinion.	90
☐ use expressions to get someone to agree with me.	91
Writing	
☐ brainstorm and organize ideas to plan an article.	93

What's up?

UNIT 10

Lesson A Catching up

1 What have they been doing?

Grammar **A What have these people been doing? What have they done? Complete the sentences using the present perfect continuous and then the present perfect.**

1. Kazuo *'s been doing yard work* (do yard work). He *'s planted* (plant) some flowers.

2. Sienna and Lynn _____________ (shop). They _____________ (spend) over $500 each!

3. Lola _____________ (run). She _________ just _________ (finish) a marathon.

4. Carmen _____________ (cook) dinner. She _____________ (grill) some fish.

5. Sal and Elena _____________ (ski). They _____________ (have) one lesson.

6. Tony _____________ (do) laundry all morning. He _____________ (wash) three loads.

B Circle the correct word to complete each sentence.

1. Kazuo's been doing yard work **since** / **for** (circled) a few hours.
2. Sienna and Lynn haven't shopped online **since** / **in** months.
3. Lola's been running **since** / **for** she was in college.
4. Carmen hasn't made unhealthy food **since** / **in** a long time.
5. Sal and Elena have been skiing **since** / **for** this morning.
6. Tony's been doing the laundry **for** / **in** over two hours.

2 Questions, questions . . .

Grammar **Read each situation. Then use the words to write questions and answers in the present perfect continuous or the present perfect.**

1. You have a friend who has been taking Spanish lessons. You ask:
   A (how long / study / Spanish) *How long have you been studying Spanish?*
   B (seven months) *I've been studying Spanish for seven months.*
   A (how many words / learn) ____________________
   B (about 250) ____________________
2. You meet a famous baseball player. You ask:
   A (how long / play / baseball) ____________________
   B (18 years) ____________________
   A (how many games / win this season) ____________________
   B (12 out of 15) ____________________

3 About you

Grammar **A Complete the questions. Use the present perfect continuous or the present perfect.**

1. What *have* you *been doing* (do) lately after class?
2. How many times __________ you __________ (go) to the movies this month?
3. Who __________ you __________ (hang out) with recently?
4. How many times __________ you __________ (eat out) at a restaurant this week?
5. __________ you __________ (study) a lot lately?
6. How many phone calls __________ you __________ (make) this week?
7. How many times __________ you __________ (oversleep) in the last month?
8. What __________ you __________ (think) about for the last hour?
9. How many books __________ you __________ (read) this year?
10. __________ you __________ (exercise) lately?

B Answer the questions in part A with true information.

1. *I've been taking guitar lessons.*
2. ____________________
3. ____________________
4. ____________________
5. ____________________
6. ____________________
7. ____________________
8. ____________________
9. ____________________
10. ____________________

1 Crossword puzzle

Vocabulary | **Complete the crossword puzzle.**

Across

2. A movie with an exciting story and lots of suspense is a *thriller* .
3. A _________ movie is about soldiers.
5. In a romantic _________ , two people fall in love and funny things happen.
7. A movie about a real event is called a _________ story.
9. A movie that makes you cry is called a tear_________ .
10. An _________ movie has a fast-moving story and is often violent.

Down

1. A _________ -fiction movie often takes place in the future.
4. A movie with cartoon characters is an _________ movie.
6. A movie that has singing and dancing is a _________ .
8. _________ movies are often scary and have monsters in them.

2 Best of Bollywood

Vocabulary | **Complete Daria's blog with the words in the box.**

✓comedies	endings	love story	set in	subtitled
costumes	hilarious	play	stunts	take place

Daria's Blog

Daria 12:31 p.m.

Some of my favorite movies are musicals from Bollywood, especially the romantic *comedies* . The movies are usually _________ _________ India, and the actors often _________ characters who fall in love. I really enjoy a good _________ _________ . They can sometimes be tearjerkers, but the nice thing about Bollywood movies is that they often have happy _________ , so you leave the movie theater feeling good. Some of them are also very funny – the last one I saw was just _________ . Some of them are historical and _________ _________ in the past. These are my favorites because the colors and the _________ are wonderful. The movies aren't usually in English, but they're _________ , so you can read while you're watching. Sometimes the movies even have fight scenes with lots of special effects and _________ . They're really great!

3 About you

Vocabulary | **Write reviews of movies you've seen. Complete each sentence with the title of a movie. Then write more about each one by answering the questions.**

CHOOSE A MOVIE	What type of movie is it? What's it about? Who's in it? Did you like it? Why? Why not?
1. I really enjoyed ______ *Les Misérables* ______ .	*It's a musical, and it's set in France in the 1800s. Hugh Jackman plays a man who escapes from prison. Russell Crowe is the police officer who chases him. I really enjoyed the movie. It has wonderful music, and the costumes are amazing.*
2. ______ ______ is playing right now.	
3. The best movie I've ever seen is ______ ______ .	
4. I didn't like ______ ______ .	

4 I still haven't see it.

Grammar and vocabulary | **Complete the conversation with *already*, *still*, or *yet*.**

Ann There are so many movies that I *still* haven't seen. Do you want to go see one tonight?

Gus Yeah, OK. Let's see. How about Brad Pitt's new movie? I haven't seen that ______.

Ann Oh, I've ______ seen that one. It was good. How about the new horror movie that's out? Have you seen that ______ ?

Gus No, I don't like scary movies. I'm 25, and I ______ haven't seen a horror movie.

Ann Well, there's a new animated movie out. I haven't seen that one ______ , either.

Gus Oh, great. Let's go. I've been dying to see it!

Lesson C I was wondering . . .

1 Favors

Conversation strategies **Complete the conversations with the expressions in the box.**

I wanted to	I was wondering,
✓ I was wondering if I could	Would it be all right if I
I was wondering if you could	Would it be OK

1. **Victor** Hi, Raoul. What can I do for you?
   Raoul *I was wondering if I could* talk to you for a moment. Is now OK?
   Victor No problem. Come on in.
   Raoul Thanks. ____________ worked from home tomorrow?
   Victor Tomorrow?
   Raoul Yes. Someone is coming to fix my stove, and I need to be home to let him in. ____________ with you?
   Victor Yeah, sure. I don't see why not.
   Raoul Thanks, Victor. I really appreciate it.

2. **Dad** Hi, Josie. What's up?
   Josie Hey, Dad. ____________ ask you a favor.
   Dad Sure, what is it?
   Josie Well, ____________ lend me some money – if that's OK.
   Dad Hmm. It depends. How much? And for what?
   Josie Well, I was thinking, your birthday is next week, right?
   Dad Yes, it is.
   Josie So, ____________ could I borrow $50 to buy you your present?

2 Can I borrow the car?

Conversation strategies

Stephanie's friend Ally is coming for a visit. Stephanie needs to ask her roommate Jenny for some favors. Look at her list, and complete each of her requests.

Things I need to do:

1. *Ask Jenny if Ally can stay here.*
2. *Pick up Ally at airport – borrow Jenny's car.*
3. *See if Jenny wants to go sightseeing with us Saturday.*
4. *Organize a party Saturday night – check with Jenny.*
5. *Check Ally's return flight online – use Jenny's computer.*

1. I wanted to *ask you if Ally could stay here*.
2. I was wondering if I could ______.
3. I was wondering, ______?
4. Would it be all right ______?
5. Would it be OK with you if I ______?

3 All right. What time?

Conversation strategies

Choose the best sentence to continue each conversation. Then write *A* if the speaker is agreeing, *M* if the speaker is moving the conversation along, or *U* to show the speaker understands.

1. A I'm going grocery shopping later, and I was wondering if you could come and help me. [*A*]
   B ☑ All right. What time?
   ☐ That's OK.

2. A Do you have time to talk now? [ ]
   B Sure. Let me just put these papers away.
   ☐ Um, OK, I guess so.
   ☐ All right. What did you want to talk about?

3. A This pasta is delicious! Could you give me the recipe? [ ]
   B ☐ Sure. It's very easy.
   ☐ That would be OK.

4. A Can you help me with something? [ ]
   B ☐ OK. What do you need?
   ☐ That's all right.

5. A I'm leaving early today. [ ]
   B ☐ Right. I remember you have an appointment.
   ☐ OK. I think so, too.

1 Weekend favorites

Reading | **A Read the reviews. What things are reviewed? Check (✓) the boxes.**

☐ a book ☐ a movie ☐ a phone app ☐ a video game ☐ a Web app

Weekend Blog

THINGS TO KEEP YOU BUSY ON WEEKENDS

1. MOVIE EFFECTIVE

With Movie Effective, you can add special effects to your videos. Simply record a video with your smartphone camera. Then add exciting effects — just like they do in the movies. The app comes with two effects — lightning and slow motion — but you can also buy others, like sound effects. Even though I don't usually shoot or share videos personally, I found this to be a lot of fun. So, be careful — it's addictive, and you may get totally hooked!

2. ACCUSED

I really enjoyed playing this game. It combines a science-fiction setting with great action. You are a character who is wrongly accused of a crime. You have to find out who the real criminal is and get justice. Your choices determine the storyline. The action is fast-moving and there are some sad moments, so if you're very sensitive, this may not be the video game for you. However, the amazing setting and the ability to create your own story make this a great game for most players.

3. RECORDYOURRUN

If you are serious about running, hiking, biking, or even skiing, and have been wondering how to keep track of your progress, this phone app is the answer. It records your pace, distance, and time, and you can save your results and compare different exercise sessions. You can set goals for each time you go out and share your progress with friends. There's also a feature that lets your friends and family follow your progress in a race on a map. This app is the perfect way to mix technology and exercise.

4. FRETENDS

FretEnds has a fabulous Web app that will teach you how to play the guitar. You can choose to play a real guitar or a virtual one. There are eight levels of play. If you start at the beginner level, you will learn to play "Brown Eyed Girl." You need to let the app access the microphone on your computer, so it can "hear" you play. Each song is broken down into small parts. After you've learned one part, you can move on. This app is great for everyone, whether you've never played or even if you've been playing for years.

B Read the article again. Write *T* (true) or *F* (false) for each sentence. Then correct the false sentences.

1. Movie Effective helps you record videos on your smartphone. F
2. The special effects on Movie Effective are all free. ____
3. *Accused* is a romantic comedy. ____
4. *Accused* is suitable for everyone. ____
5. RecordYourRun is for people who take exercise seriously. ____
6. With RecordYourRun, people can see if their friends are winning a race. ____
7. You need to buy a guitar before you can use the FretEnds app. ____
8. The FretEnds app is not for experienced players. ____

2 Music review

Writing | **A** Read the music review. Complete the sentences with *although*, *even though*, or *even if* to contrast ideas. Sometimes more than one answer is possible.

___________ *Come Away With Me* was amazingly successful and really introduced Norah Jones to the world, *Little Broken Hearts* is a much better album. Most of her earlier work uses a lot of piano, but this album focuses more on the guitar, so the sound is different. ___________ most of these songs are about heartbreak, the music is beautiful and sweet. ___________ you don't like sad romantic songs, you will find something to enjoy in this new collection.

– *Music Scene* magazine

B Write a review of a movie, an album, or a TV show. Use *although*, *even though*, and *even if* to contrast ideas.

Unit 10 Progress chart

	What can you do? Mark the boxes. ✓ = I can . . . ? = I need to review how to . . .	To review, go back to these pages in the Student's Book.
Grammar	☐ use the present perfect and present perfect continuous.	98 and 99
	☐ use *since*, *for*, and *in* with the present perfect to show duration.	99
	☐ use *already*, *still*, and *yet* with the present perfect.	101
Vocabulary	☐ name at least 6 different kinds of movies.	100 and 101
	☐ talk about movies using at least 15 new words and expressions.	100 and 101
Conversation strategies	☐ ask for a favor politely.	102
	☐ use *All right*, *OK*, and *Sure* to agree to requests; *All right*, *OK*, and *So* to move a conversation to a new phase or topic; and *Right* to show I agree or understand.	103
Writing	☐ use *although*, *even though*, and *even if* to contrast ideas.	105

Impressions

UNIT 11

Lesson A Speculating

1 It could be . . .

Grammar | **Complete the sentences with the expressions in the box. Then write a second sentence using the cues and an appropriate modal.**

can't be the winners	may be taking a driving test	✓must be learning to drive
could be taking a hard test	might be the best student	must be the winners

1. He *must be learning to drive* .
   It could / might / may be his first lesson.
   (It / be / his first lesson)
2. He ______________________ .
   ____
   (It / be / his first lesson)

3. She ______________________ .
   ____
   (She / feel proud)
4. She ______________________ .
   ____
   (She / be nervous)

5. They ______________________ .
   ____
   (They / practice a lot)
6. They ______________________ .
   ____
   (They / be disappointed)

2 He must be crazy!

Grammar | **Circle the correct words to complete the sentences.**

1. Mandy What's he doing? He **must be** / **can't be** crazy!
   Molly He **might be** / **can't be** an acrobat with the circus.
   Mandy You're right. He **must practice** / **must be practicing** for tonight's show.
   Molly That's amazing! I mean, it **can't be** / **might be** easy to bend like that.
   Mandy Yeah, it **could be** / **must not be** painful, too.
   Molly Well, I certainly won't try that!

2. Jason How old is that kid? She **must be** / **can't be** more than five years old.
   Peter Yeah, you're right. She **must not be** / **might be** about four or five.
   Jason She's really good. She **must play** / **must be playing** every day for hours and hours.
   Peter She makes it look so easy, too. I wonder what her parents think. They **could be** / **must be** so proud.
   Jason Yeah, she **could be** / **can't be** the youngest professional piano player in the world.

3 About you

Grammar | **Think of someone you know who is not in the room with you now. Answer the questions about him or her using *must*, *may*, *might*, *could*, or *can't*.**

1. Where do you think he or she is right now?
   It's Saturday afternoon, so he might be on the golf course. He can't be at work.
2. What do you think he or she is doing?
   ____
3. How do you think he or she is feeling?
   ____
4. What do you think he or she is wearing?
   ____
5. Who do you think he or she is with?
   ____
6. What do you think he or she is thinking about right now?
   ____

1 Scrambled up

Grammar and vocabulary

A Write the adjective for each definition. You can check your answers in a dictionary. Then use the letters in the boxes to answer the question below.

1. Greatly surprised a m [a] z e d
2. Upset or not pleased __ __ [ ] __ __ __ __
3. Makes you feel excited __ [ ] __ __ __ __ __ __
4. Irritating __ __ __ __ __ __ __ __ __ [ ] __ __
5. Not interesting __ [ ] __ __ __ __
6. Not expected or normal __ [ ] __ __ __ __ __ __ __ __
7. Frightening [ ] __ __ __ __

How might you feel the first time you try something new? a __ __ __ __ __ __ __

B Complete the sentences with the other forms of the adjectives in part A.

1. Someone who upsets you or makes you slightly angry is annoying .
2. If someone gives you a present for no reason, you might be ________ .
3. If you have nothing to do, you might feel ________ .
4. When you're very afraid of something, you might feel ________ .
5. Someone who learns to speak six or seven languages is truly ________ .
6. When you're going to do something fun, you are ________ about it.
7. When you can't remember a word in English, you probably feel ________ .

2 Good news, bad news

Grammar and vocabulary | **Complete the emails. Use the correct forms of the adjectives.**

New Message

To: EmmaP@cup.com
From: shak91@cup.com
Subject: My short story

Hey Emma,

I'm so _excited_ (excite). Remember the short story I wrote for English class last month? Well, my teacher sent it to a competition, and guess what? It won first prize! The judges said my story was very ________ (interest). I knew my teacher was ________ (please) with my work. She said my story was ________ (fascinate). But I never thought she would enter it in a competition! I was totally ________ (shock) when she told me. And all my classmates were totally ________ (jealous). What's new and exciting with you?

Shakira

New Message

To: shak91@cup.com
From: EmmaP@cup.com
Subject: My short story

Hi Shakira,

Congratulations! I wish I had ________ (excite) news for you, too, but I don't. Unfortunately, I failed my driver's test last week. I was really ________ (disappoint). It's just so ________ (embarrass) – it's the third time I've failed the test. The driving instructor told me to make a right-hand turn, and I turned left instead. I guess I got a little ________ (confuse). I could tell the instructor was really ________ (annoy) with me! My dad told me not to get ________ (frustrate). He said he failed his driver's test five times before he finally passed, but I'm starting to get ________ (worry). Well, talk to you later.

Emma

3 About you

Grammar and vocabulary | **How would you feel in these situations? Complete the sentences with true information.**

1. You fail a test that you have studied very hard for.
   I would feel _disappointed if I failed a test that I thought I was prepared for_.
   It might be _embarrassing if my friends found out_.
2. Your friend doesn't show up for a date.
   I would get ________________________________.
   I might feel ________________________________.
3. You are home alone during a storm.
   I might feel ________________________________.
   It could be ________________________________.
4. Someone is telling you a story you've already heard ten times.
   I might feel ________________________________.
   I would probably think ________________________________.

1 You must be excited.

Conversation strategies **Complete the responses in the conversations to show understanding. Use *must be* and an adjective.**

1. I'm learning how to design a website. — *That must be hard* .
2. My brother always takes my stuff. — That ______________________.
3. I lost my wallet and credit cards at the mall. — You ______________________.
4. I'm going to climb Mount Rainier next month. — You ______________________.
5. I didn't win the poetry contest. — You ______________________.
6. My ex-boyfriend is dating my best friend. — That ______________________.

2 Explanations

Conversation strategies **Complete the conversation with *you see* or *I see*, or leave a blank where neither one is appropriate.**

Walt Hi, Reg. I'm sorry I'm late. I didn't hear my alarm. *You see* , I was working on my report until about 3:30 this morning.

Reg Uh-huh, ____________ . So, will it be ready for the meeting with the boss?

Walt ____________ Yes. I just have to make some copies. What time is the meeting?

Reg Well, it was at 11:00, but the boss called me about half an hour ago, and it's now at 2:30. She's meeting someone for lunch, ____________ , and she has to leave at 11:30.

Walt Oh, ____________ . So, I guess I didn't have to rush.

Reg Well, at least it's all done now, and you can relax.

3 An author in Paris

Conversation strategies | **Complete the conversation with the expressions in the box. Use each expression twice.**

I see	that must be	you must be	you see

Akina Hey, Omar. I hear you're going away for a while. Where to?

Omar Yeah, I'm leaving for Paris next week.

Akina You're kidding! Wow, _you must be_ excited!

Omar I am. I've never been there before. ____________, I'm going to do some research for my next book. That's always the best part – the research.

Akina I bet. ____________ fun. So, what's your book about?

Omar It's a love story, of course.

Akina ____________. Uh . . . can you share any details yet?

Omar I guess. Hmm . . . let's see. It's about a young girl who goes to visit a friend in Paris. And well, you know, she meets a mysterious young man, they fall in love, and lots of things happen.

Akina Really? What kind of things?

Omar Well, I don't want to say yet. ____________, I want to keep the details a surprise.

Akina I understand. But, gosh, ____________ hard. I can never keep secrets.

Omar I know what you mean. It's difficult sometimes.

Akina So, tell me what else you're doing in Paris.

Omar Oh. I'm going to read from my last novel at an English-language bookstore.

Akina Great! ____________ pleased about that. Will you be nervous?

Omar No, not at all. I've done it several times. It's part of the job of being a writer.

Akina ____________. Well, have a wonderful trip. Good luck with your research.

Omar Thanks. I'll tell you all about it when I get back.

1 Child prodigies

Reading | **A Read the article. What does "child prodigy" mean?**

☐ someone under the age of 15 ☐ a child with a special talent ☐ a child who is famous

CHILD PRODIGIES: Nature OR Nurture?

Mozart wrote his first minuet at age six. Cellist Yo-Yo Ma first performed in public at the age of five. William James Sidis read Homer in Greek at age four and was the youngest person ever to attend Harvard University at 11. Ukrainian chess player Sergey Karjakin became the youngest international grand master at 12. Pablo Picasso first publicly exhibited his paintings at age 13.

Many parents may hope for a genius child, but there can be a price to pay. Some child prodigies never experience a normal childhood, often because it's difficult for them to make friends, and they suffer socially. Some genius children even have mental breakdowns at an early age, and gifted child athletes or musicians can be permanently injured from practicing too hard.

We often hear stories of parents who push their children too hard. However, some experts say that for the most part, "pushy parent" is an unfair label: Parents don't push prodigies, prodigies push parents. Many gifted children quickly become bored with school and homework that is too easy. For these kids, school is frustrating, and they risk losing interest in it altogether. It's better to allow these children to skip grades, experts say, than to let them become disappointed in school.

Are prodigies born, or are they created? The short answer is: we don't know. Certainly, many parents of gifted children provide a stimulating environment: They read to their children at an early age, take them to museums and concerts, and give them a lot of independence. But experts advise parents not to be disappointed if their child isn't an early genius. Mozart was a child prodigy; Einstein was not. But the world is still amazed by them both.

B Find a word or expression in the article for each meaning below.

1. go to, or be present at (a place or an event) (paragraph 1) _attend_
2. psychological problems (paragraph 2) ________
3. talented; exceptional (paragraph 3) ________
4. interesting; encouraging you to learn (paragraph 4) ________

C Read the article again. Then answer the questions.

1. Who's the youngest prodigy mentioned in the article?

____

2. What are three disadvantages of being a child prodigy?

____

3. What problems do some gifted children have with school?

____

4. How do some parents help their gifted children develop?

____

2 My child is a prodigy!

Writing

A **Read the letter from a parent to a school principal. Circle the expressions that give impressions or opinions. Underline the statements that are stated as fact.**

MT

Dear Dr. Evans,

My child is enrolled in your school. I believe that he is a very gifted student, and I feel that he is bored in his classes. It seems to me that he is becoming increasingly frustrated and anxious because he has lost interest in school. Last year he was the top student in his class, but this year his grades are slipping. My impression is that he needs to take more difficult classes. In my opinion, he is not finding his current classes challenging enough. Can you help?

Sincerely,

Marsha Taylor

B **Write a letter to the editor of a local newspaper about one of the topics below or your own idea. Use the expressions from part A.**

- There aren't enough leisure facilities for local teens.
- We need healthier food options in schools.
- There's too much litter on city streets.

Unit 11 Progress chart

	What can you do? Mark the boxes. ✓ = I can . . . ? = I need to review how to . . .	To review, go back to these pages in the Student's Book.
Grammar	☐ use the modals *must*, *may*, *might*, *can't*, and *could* to speculate.	108 and 109
	☐ use adjectives ending in *-ed* to describe how someone feels.	110 and 111
	☐ use adjectives ending in *-ing* to describe someone or something.	110 and 111
Vocabulary	☐ name at least 12 adjectives to describe feelings and reactions.	110 and 111
Conversation strategies	☐ use *That must be* or *You must be* + adjective to show I understand.	112
	☐ use *You see* to explain something and *I see* to show I understand.	113
Writing	☐ use expressions like *I feel* to give impressions or opinions.	115

In the news

UNIT 12

Lesson A / Local news

1 And now, the news . . .

Grammar | **Complete the news reports. Use the simple past passive.**

1. Newtown Park train station _was closed_ (close) this morning after a bag ____________ (find) on a train. Several trains ____________ (delay), and some ____________ (cancel). The bag ____________ (remove) from the station and ____________ (search). Police said later that the bag was full of clothes. The train station ____________ (reopen) after two hours.

2. A woman ____________ (rescue) earlier today after she climbed onto her roof to repair her chimney. Firefighters ____________ (call) to the scene after neighbors heard the woman shout for help. Fortunately, the woman ____________ (not hurt), but she ____________ (take) to the local hospital and ____________ (release) later this afternoon.

3. The National Museum ____________ (break into) last night, and three valuable paintings ____________ (steal). The area around the museum ____________ (close off) following the incident, and bystanders ____________ (interview). Police are now looking for two young men who ____________ (see) nearby.

2 More news

Grammar | **Rewrite the sentences using the simple past passive.**

1. They delayed the game for two hours. *The game was delayed for two hours.*
2. Someone stole a ring from an exhibit. ____________________
3. They canceled the rock concert. ____________________
4. A woman found a wallet on a bus. ____________________
5. They took two people to the hospital. ____________________
6. Someone rescued a man from a fire. ____________________

3 What happened?

Grammar | **Look at the picture. What do you think happened? Write a news report. Use the verbs in the box or your own ideas. Use the simple past passive. Be creative with your facts!**

break into
close
find
hurt
open
rob
steal
take

News Report: Stolen Goods!

A downtown jewelry store was robbed yesterday.

Lesson B Natural disasters

1 All kinds of weather

Vocabulary | **Look at the pictures. Complete the sentences with the words in the box.**

aftershocks	floods	hurricane	✓rains	tornado
earthquake	hailstorm	lightning	thunderstorm	winds

1. The region was hit by heavy ___rains___ earlier today. Several roads were closed because of flash ______________ .

2. Farmers say their crops were badly damaged by the ice from a freak ______________ that passed through the area today.

3. Parts of the country were damaged by a ______________ yesterday.

4. Airports were closed today due to ______________ Albert. Flights were canceled because of strong ______________ and rain.

5. The area was hit yesterday by a major ______________ , measuring 5.6 on the Richter scale. ______________ were felt throughout the area.

6. Electricity throughout the city was disrupted by thunder and ______________ from a severe ______________ .

2 What was the cause?

Grammar and vocabulary | **Look at each pair of pictures. What caused the damage? Write a sentence using the given word and *by*.**

1. *A fire was started by a candle.*

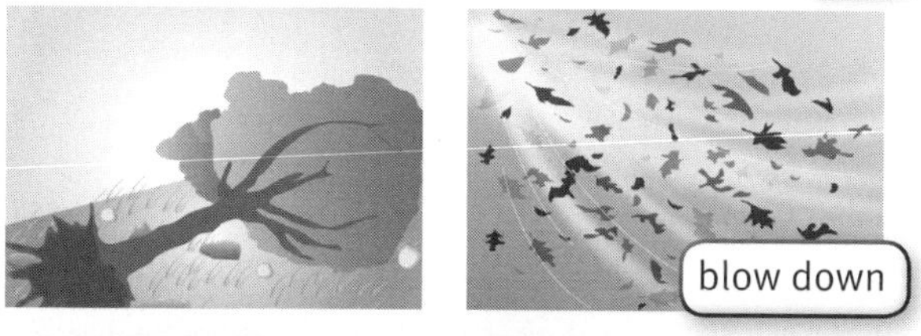

2. ______________________

3. ______________________

4. ______________________

5. ______________________

3 In the news

Grammar | **Rewrite the sentences using the simple past passive and the adverb given.**

1. The fire damaged the building. (partially)
   The building was partially damaged by the fire.
2. The storm disrupted train services. (temporarily)
   ____
3. Flash floods damaged several houses in the area. (badly)
   ____
4. A wildfire injured three firefighters. (seriously)
   ____
5. A tornado destroyed a small farm. (completely)
   ____

Lesson C Did you hear about . . . ?

1 News travels fast!

Conversation strategies **Complete the conversation with the expressions in the box. Use each expression only once.**

did I tell you	guess what	you know
did you hear about	✓have you heard	you know what

Don *Have you heard* the news about Henry?

Nadia No. What happened to him?

Don Well, ______________ he goes mountain biking, right?

Nadia Yes. I've seen him on his bike a lot.

Don Well, he went out biking yesterday, and ______________? He was in the mountains during that big thunderstorm in the afternoon. He had to sit under a tree to avoid the lightning. . . .

Nadia Under a tree? ______________? That's really dangerous.

Don It is?

Nadia Oh, yeah. ______________ those golfers who were hit by lightning under a tree?

Don No. Oh, that's awful.

Nadia Yeah. They were taken to the hospital and everything. But amazingly, they were OK.

Don That was lucky. By the way, ______________ about my car? The roof was damaged in that storm, too. It was hit by the hailstones.

2 About you

Conversation strategies **Write sentences introducing some news. Use true information.**

1. *You know my friend Callie? She got a new laptop for her birthday.*
(good news about a friend)
2. ______________
(fun news about yourself)
3. ______________
(bad news about a local sports team)
4. ______________
(news about the local weather)
5. ______________
(interesting news about your favorite actor or singer)
6. ______________
(news about a family member)
7. ______________
(news about another city)

3 The funny thing was . . .

Conversation strategies

Circle the best way to complete each sentence.

1. I lost my bag last week, and then I found it outside my dorm room. The funny thing was, **everything was stolen** / **nothing was stolen**.
2. Thieves broke into my car last week, and the worst thing was, **they took my favorite bag** / **the inside of the car was completely cleaned**.
3. Some neighbors of ours got married last month, and the weird thing is, **they didn't tell anyone about it** / **we all had a great time**.
4. We had a great weekend at the beach. The best thing was, **the water was so warm** / **it rained**.
5. That movie was incredible. The only thing was, **the ending was the best** / **the ending was disappointing**.
6. We went out for dinner last night, and the food was terrible. The other thing was, **the waiters were helpful** / **it was really expensive**.

4 The whole story

Conversation strategies

Complete the conversations with the expressions in the box.

Did I tell you?	The best thing is,
✓Did you hear	The funny thing is,

1. A *Did you hear* about the new vacation schedule?
   B No, I didn't. What about it?
   A We get an extra week of vacation.
   B Great!
   A ________________ the extra week is in February. That means we can plan a nice, long ski vacation!

2. A ________________ There was a small fire at school yesterday.
   B Really? Where?
   A It was in the science lab. Some students were doing an experiment, and it exploded.
   B I hope no one was hurt.
   A Everyone is fine. ________________ the students all got A's!

Lesson D Reporting the news

1 Only the news that interests you

Reading **A Read the article. Which news sources do young people use?**

CHANGING SOURCES OF NEWS

Far fewer people, especially the young, get their news from traditional news sources (either print or television), according to the most recent surveys. Instead, they are getting news from online sources and social networking sites, using their cell phones, tablets, and other mobile devices. In just two years, the number of people who get news from social networks doubled, and now about a third of young readers get their news this way. Although half of all Americans still watch TV to keep up with events, only 28% of people between the ages of 18 and 29 do so.

This use of social networks for news can be seen in Europe also. One in five people in the United Kingdom, and 43% of young people, get their news from the most popular social networking and microblogging sites. According to a recent study in Spain, three-quarters of the people between the ages of 16 and 30 got their news from a social networking site, as compared to only 28% from newspapers.

The addition of these news channels may contribute to "news fatigue," or a feeling of being overloaded with news. A study that was conducted by the University of Texas found that the way we get the news affects whether we feel information overload. People who got their news from computers and tablets were much more likely to feel overloaded, while people who got their news from TV or read it on their cell phone were less likely to experience this. The study showed that reading the same news on a computer was felt to be more tiring than reading it on a phone, perhaps because options seem more limited on a phone, and so more manageable. People on computers and tablets usually see many more links than people who use phone apps.

News organizations have adapted their news presentation style to try to prevent or reduce news fatigue. Some provide news in three forms: breaking headlines, short present-tense stories, and links to longer stories. By cutting down the number of headline updates, they also hope to reduce news fatigue.

B Read the article again. Circle the best alternatives to complete the sentences.

1. The author suggests in the article that young people and older people ____.
   a. get news the same way (b.) often get their news from different sources
2. One news source that is growing in popularity is ____.
   a. microblogging sites b. television news
3. Three out of four young people get their news from social networks in ____.
   a. Spain b. the United States
4. People who get their news on computers are more likely to be overloaded than if they get their news on ____.
   a. tablets b. smartphones
5. One way that people get news fatigue is by reading too many ____.
   a. headline updates b. longer stories

2 News survey

Writing **A Read the survey. Then complete the article below with the expressions in the box.**

***Barnesville News* Survey:**

1. Do you read the *Barnesville News* every day? **Yes** 49% **No** 51%
2. What's your favorite section?

Section	%
Weather	0%
Local	9%
Sports	10%
Arts	20%
International	59%
Travel	2%

almost
✓half
majority
none
out of
20%

About ___half___ of the people we surveyed read the *Barnesville News* every day. The ________ of *Barnesville News* readers prefer the international section. Only one ________ ten readers chose the sports section as their favorite. ________ 10% of readers enjoy the local section, while ________ of them are interested in the arts section. ________ of them chose the weather as their favorite.

B How many of your friends read a local or national news website? Write a paragraph like the one in part A to show the statistics.

Unit 12 Progress chart

	What can you do? Mark the boxes. ✓ = I can . . . ? = I need to review how to . . .	To review, go back to these pages in the Student's Book.
Grammar	☐ use the simple past passive to discuss the news.	118, 119, and 120
	☐ use the passive + *by* to introduce the "doer" or cause of an action.	120 and 121
Vocabulary	☐ name at least 10 types of extreme weather or natural disasters.	120 and 121
	☐ name at least 4 adverbs with the simple past passive.	120 and 121
Conversation strategies	☐ introduce news with expressions like *Guess what?*	122
	☐ use expressions like *The thing is . . .* to introduce issues.	123
Writing	☐ write about statistics.	125

Illustration credits

Harry Briggs: 22, 42, 80 **Cambridge University Press:** 21, 50 **Steve Cancel:** 93 **Chuck Gonzales:** 13, 37, 58, 82, 83 **Frank Montagna:** 2, 26, 27, 44, 67, 86, 87 **Marilena Perilli:** 6, 7, 20, 28, 46, 62, 63, 74 **Greg White:** 14, 35, 78, 91 **Terry Wong:** 5, 38, 39, 54, 68, 69, 94, 95

Photo credits

3 ©Andresr/Shutterstock **4** ©Erin Patrice O'Brien/Getty **8** *(top to bottom)* ©Michael Tran/FilmMagic/Getty Images; ©Eros International/courtesy Everett Collection **9** ©Monirul Alam/ZUMAPRESS.com/Alamy **10** *(left to right)* ©Alexandra Lande/Shutterstock; ©GoodSportHD.com/Alamy **11** ©Eyecandy Images/Alamy **12** *(top to bottom)* ©Yadid Levy/age fotostock/SuperStock; ©Andrew Bain/Getty Images; ©Manfred Grebler/Getty Images; ©Universal Images Group/SuperStock **15** *(left to right)* ©Philip Lee Harvey/Getty Images; ©Punchstock **16** *(top to bottom)* ©Oktay Ortakcioglu/Getty Images; ©leungchopan/Shutterstock **18** *(top row, left to right)* ©Francesco Dazzi/Shutterstock; ©Medioimages/Photodisc/Thinkstock; ©Maurilio Cheli/Associated Press; ©Max Nash/Associated Press *(bottom row, left to right)* ©Jerritt Clark/WireImage/Getty Images; ©Randy Faris/Corbis; ©Alik Keplicz/Associated Press; ©Mike Segar/Reuters/Newscom **19** ©Andrzej Gorzkowski Photography/Alamy **20** *(clockwise from top left)* ©Punchstock; ©Thinkstock; ©Digital Vision/Thinkstock; ©Thinkstock; ©AAMIR QURESHI/AFP/Getty Images; ©Galen Rowell/Corbis **23** ©Thinkstock **24** ©Photo Courtesy of NOAA *(background)* ©Serg Zastavkin/Shutterstock *(icicles)* ©April Cat/Shutterstock **25** ©Thinkstock **29** ©imagebroker.net/SuperStock **32** ©Frank Herholdt/Getty Images **34** ©George Kerrigan **35** ©George Kerrigan **36** *(top to bottom)* ©ifong/Shutterstock; ©Stockvision/Shutterstock **40** ©Thinkstock **41** *(top to bottom)* ©Robyn Mackenzie/Shutterstock; ©Lucky Business/Shutterstock **50** *(top to bottom)* ©Thinkstock; ©Punchstock; ©Dennis MacDonald/Age Fotostock; ©Sherrianne Talon/istockphoto; ©Jurgen Reisch/Getty Images **53** ©Rich Legg/Getty Images **55** *(all photos)* ©Thinkstock **59** ©x7vector/Shutterstock **61** ©Andrew D. Bernstein/NBAE via Getty Images **62** ©John Giustina/Getty Images **66** ©MediaBakery **70** ©PBS/Courtesy: Everett Collection **75** ©Clark Brennan/Alamy **77** ©Jupiterimages/Thinkstock **80** *(top)* ©DircinhaSW/Getty Images *(bottom, left to right)* ©JGI/Getty Images/RF; ©Cultura Limited/SuperStock **81** ©David Wolff-Patrick/WireImage/Getty Images **84** *(clockwise from top left)* ©Punchstock; ©Nick Chaldakov/Alamy; ©Thinkstock; ©Digital Vision/Thinkstock **90** *(top to bottom)* ©Mike Finn-Kelcey/Newscom; ©RubberBall/SuperStock; ©Thinkstock **92** *(clockwise from top left)* ©Sandra Mu/Getty Images; ©David Cole/Alamy; ©Thinkstock; ©Thinkstock; ©Thinkstock; ©Eric Nguyen/Jim Reed Photography/Corbis

Text credits

While every effort has been made, it has not always been possible to identify the sources of all the materials used, or to trace all copyright holders. If any omissions are brought to our notice, we will be happy to include the appropriate acknowledgements on reprinting.

The top 500 spoken words

This is a list of the top 500 words in spoken North American English. It is based on a sample of four and a half million words of conversation from the Cambridge International Corpus. The most frequent word, *I*, is at the top of the list.

1. I
2. and
3. the
4. you
5. uh
6. to
7. a
8. that
9. it
10. of
11. yeah
12. know
13. in
14. like
15. they
16. have
17. so
18. was
19. but
20. is
21. it's
22. we
23. huh
24. just
25. oh
26. do
27. don't
28. that's
29. well
30. for
31. what
32. on
33. think
34. right
35. not
36. um
37. or
38. my
39. be
40. really
41. with
42. he
43. one
44. are
45. this
46. there
47. I'm
48. all
49. if
50. no
51. get
52. about
53. at
54. out
55. had
56. then
57. because
58. go
59. up
60. she
61. when
62. them
63. can
64. would
65. as
66. me
67. mean
68. some
69. good
70. got
71. OK
72. people
73. now
74. going
75. were
76. lot
77. your
78. time
79. see
80. how
81. they're
82. kind
83. here
84. from
85. did
86. something
87. too
88. more
89. very
90. want
91. little
92. been
93. things
94. an
95. you're
96. said
97. there's
98. I've
99. much
100. where
101. two
102. thing
103. her
104. didn't
105. other
106. say
107. back
108. could
109. their
110. our
111. guess
112. yes
113. way
114. has
115. down
116. we're
117. any

The top 500 spoken words

118. he's
119. work
120. take
121. even
122. those
123. over
124. probably
125. him
126. who
127. put
128. years
129. sure
130. can't
131. pretty
132. gonna
133. stuff
134. come
135. these
136. by
137. into
138. went
139. make
140. than
141. year
142. three
143. which
144. home
145. will
146. nice
147. never
148. only
149. his
150. doing
151. cause
152. off
153. I'll
154. maybe
155. real
156. why
157. big
158. actually
159. she's
160. day
161. five
162. always
163. school
164. look
165. still
166. around
167. anything
168. kids
169. first
170. does
171. need
172. us
173. should
174. talking
175. last
176. thought
177. doesn't
178. different
179. money
180. long
181. used
182. getting
183. same
184. four
185. every
186. new
187. everything
188. many
189. before
190. though
191. most
192. tell
193. being
194. bit
195. house
196. also
197. use
198. through
199. feel
200. course
201. what's
202. old
203. done
204. sort
205. great
206. bad
207. we've
208. another
209. car
210. true
211. whole
212. whatever
213. twenty
214. after
215. ever
216. find
217. care
218. better
219. hard
220. haven't
221. trying
222. give
223. I'd
224. problem
225. else
226. remember
227. might
228. again
229. pay
230. try
231. place
232. part
233. let
234. keep
235. children
236. anyway
237. came
238. six
239. family
240. wasn't
241. talk
242. made
243. hundred
244. night
245. call
246. saying

The top 500 spoken words

247. dollars
248. live
249. away
250. either
251. read
252. having
253. far
254. watch
255. week
256. mhm
257. quite
258. enough
259. next
260. couple
261. own
262. wouldn't
263. ten
264. interesting
265. am
266. sometimes
267. bye
268. seems
269. heard
270. goes
271. called
272. point
273. ago
274. while
275. fact
276. once
277. seen
278. wanted
279. isn't
280. start
281. high
282. somebody
283. let's
284. times
285. guy
286. area
287. fun
288. they've
289. you've
290. started
291. job
292. says
293. play
294. usually
295. wow
296. exactly
297. took
298. few
299. child
300. thirty
301. buy
302. person
303. working
304. half
305. looking
306. someone
307. coming
308. eight
309. love
310. everybody
311. able
312. we'll
313. life
314. may
315. both
316. type
317. end
318. least
319. told
320. saw
321. college
322. ones
323. almost
324. since
325. days
326. couldn't
327. gets
328. guys
329. god
330. country
331. wait
332. yet
333. believe
334. thinking
335. funny
336. state
337. until
338. husband
339. idea
340. name
341. seven
342. together
343. each
344. hear
345. help
346. nothing
347. parents
348. room
349. today
350. makes
351. stay
352. mom
353. sounds
354. change
355. understand
356. such
357. gone
358. system
359. comes
360. thank
361. show
362. thousand
363. left
364. friends
365. class
366. already
367. eat
368. small
369. boy
370. paper
371. world
372. best
373. water
374. myself
375. run

The top 500 spoken words

376. they'll
377. won't
378. movie
379. cool
380. news
381. number
382. man
383. basically
384. nine
385. enjoy
386. bought
387. whether
388. especially
389. taking
390. sit
391. book
392. fifty
393. months
394. women
395. month
396. found
397. side
398. food
399. looks
400. summer
401. hmm
402. fine
403. hey
404. student
405. agree
406. mother
407. problems
408. city
409. second
410. definitely
411. spend
412. happened
413. hours
414. war
415. matter
416. supposed
417. worked
418. company
419. friend
420. set
421. minutes
422. morning
423. between
424. music
425. close
426. leave
427. wife
428. knew
429. pick
430. important
431. ask
432. hour
433. deal
434. mine
435. reason
436. credit
437. dog
438. group
439. turn
440. making
441. American
442. weeks
443. certain
444. less
445. must
446. dad
447. during
448. lived
449. forty
450. air
451. government
452. eighty
453. wonderful
454. seem
455. wrong
456. young
457. places
458. girl
459. happen
460. sorry
461. living
462. drive
463. outside
464. bring
465. easy
466. stop
467. percent
468. hand
469. gosh
470. top
471. cut
472. computer
473. tried
474. gotten
475. mind
476. business
477. anybody
478. takes
479. aren't
480. question
481. rather
482. twelve
483. phone
484. program
485. without
486. moved
487. gave
488. yep
489. case
490. looked
491. certainly
492. talked
493. beautiful
494. card
495. walk
496. married
497. anymore
498. you'll
499. middle
500. tax